"Kevin Freeman is an intense thinke~~r~~
your understanding regarding the ve~~ry real enemies of America.~~

—BEN SHAPIRO host of *The Ben Shapiro Show*

"This is a must read for every freedom-loving person on the planet."

—MICHAEL T. FLYNN Honorable LTG, USA (R)

"This groundbreaking analysis is a must-read and should be on the bookshelves of every home, classroom, and library."

—NICK ADAMS CEO of FLAG

"*According to Plan* clearly explains the battle, names our attackers, and provides a plan for Liberty to triumph."

—BOB MCEWEN Former Member of Congress

"*According to Plan,* provides clear-eyed warnings regarding both foreign and domestic enemies and how we must counter them. I strongly recommend this book."

—GLENN P. STORY Founder & CEO, Patriot Mobile

"The enemies of America are working hard to destroy the Liberty we now enjoy. This book has the action-plan solution. A must read and must share."

—NICK VUJICIC Evangelist, Influencer & Entrepreneur

"Kevin Freeman's *According to Plan* lights up the dark and hidden agenda with a beacon of truth. I heartily recommend this book to every Patriot."

—JIM DEMINT Former U.S. Senator

"*According to Plan* is a MUST read for all patriots. Learn the who, how and why, behind what we are experiencing and more importantly learn what we can do to fight back."

—PASTOR PAUL BLAIR Liberty Pastors Network

"Time is short. This is our battle cry!"

—MICHELE BACHMANN Dean and Professor, Robertson School of Government

"We Americans must read this book and respond before we lose our nation. I am honored to be able to recommend this great read to you."

—KEN ELDRED *The Integrated Life*

"My hope is that enough people will hear Kevin before it is too late."

—PHIL ROBERTSON "Duck Dynasty"

"This book has our action-plan solution. Buy one for yourself and five more as gifts."

—**KEVIN SORBO** Actor, Director, Producer, Author

"Kevin Freeman lays out the clear case that the current attack is an intentional one against the very foundations that make America great."

—**KELLY SHACKELFORD** President/CEO, First Liberty Institute

"This book must be read and must be shared."

—**DR. EVERETT PIPER** *Washington Times* Columnist

"My friend Kevin Freeman has nailed it with truth. Read this book to uncover the plan and learn how we must combat it."

—**THE HONORABLE KENNETH BLACKWELL** Former Treasurer of State of Ohio

"The Left is going to come unhinged when *According To Plan* sweeps the nation."

—**JAKE HOFFMAN** Arizona House of Representatives

"Author Kevin Freeman is an expert guide to share with you the challenges we face from the faceless elite bent on the destruction of America."

—**FLOYD BROWN** Founder of The Western Journal

"This is certainly a timely read."

—**LIEUTENANT COLONEL ALLEN B. WEST [US ARMY, RETIRED]**
Member, 112th US Congress, Former Chairman, Republican Party of Texas

"Far from theory, this book documents proven facts. Tell others or buy them copies!"

—**SAM SORBO** Author, Podcast Host, Writer, Producer and Actor

"It is important that we read *According to Plan* to learn how to combat the enemy's efforts with a plan of our own."

—**DR. JIM GARLOW** CEO, Well Versed

"To uncover the hostile and intricate plans of tyrants requires close attention for years. Kevin Freeman spent those years, and now he shows us what he has learned in this clear, readable, and frightening book."

—**DR. LARRY ARNN** President, Hillsdale College

"Awful things are happening in the world right now that are all part of a plan. It takes courage to lay it all out. Freeman says the quiet part out loud. Give it a read."

—DAVE BRAT Former Congressman, M.Div. Princeton Seminary, PH.D. Economics American U.

"Kevin Freeman is a master of clear-eyed threat analysis, helping us see behind the veil of mainstream media subterfuge."

—MAJOR GENERAL BOB DEES, U.S. ARMY, RETIRED CEO, National Center for Healthy Veterans

"We must be willing to defend our freedoms. This book helps us fight wisely and effectively by educating every American to see and understand our enemy's plan."

—STEVE KWAST Lieutenant General (Ret) USAF

"*According to Plan* is a must read for anyone who wants to understand the battle at hand and how we can win it."

—DAVE KUBAL President, Intercessors for America

"Kevin Freeman is like EF Hutton—and for good reason: People listen because he has one of the most incisive and creative minds in America."

—FRANK J. GAFFNEY Executive Chairman, Center for Security Policy

"As I constantly tell many folks, Kevin Freeman knows stuff and, thankfully, he shares much of it in this incredible book. Read it!"

—ART ALLY President, Timothy Plan Family of Biblically-based Mutual Funds

"*According To Plan* provides evidence that answers a burning question: Is America's rapid destruction on so many fronts the byproduct of ideological madness, incompetence, or worse yet—a plan?"

—DR. LANCE WALLNAU CEO Lance Learning Group

"Kevin Freeman brilliantly documents how, far from 'incompetent,' the Left's well-fueled engine is methodically demoralizing human lives, cultures, and nations."

—KELLY M. KULLBERG Editor and co-author of award-winning, *Finding God at Harvard: Spiritual Journeys of Thinking Christians*, Advisor for AmericanEvangelicals.org (AAE)

Please visit *AccordingToPlanBook.com* to see additional and full endorsements.

ACCORDING To PLAN

THE ELITES' SECRET PLAN TO SABOTAGE AMERICA

KEVIN D. FREEMAN

This book is dedicated to "He who proclaims true Liberty" (Isaiah 61:1), a cause worthy of our lives, our fortunes, and our sacred honor.

NOTE TO READERS: If the cover art of this book looks familiar to you, it's intentional. The image is modeled on the iconic cover of *1984*, the cautionary tale in which George Orwell warned us about what some are trying to do to America right now. I hope this book can be as effective a clarion call for freedom as Orwell's classic has been.

(Original cover credit undetermined. Adapted for several versions.) I also anticipate leftists will try to dismiss this book as a conspiracy theory, rather than concede it is a researched compilation of deeply troubling facts. To help you fend off such unfounded criticism, I have compiled extensive background materials, all of which you can find at AccordingToPlanBook.com/resources.

Freedom is never more than one generation away from extinction. We didn't pass it to our children in the bloodstream. It must be fought for, protected, and handed on for them to do the same, or one day we will spend our sunset years telling our children and our children's children what it was once like in the United States where men were free.

—PRESIDENT RONALD REAGAN

For our struggle is not against flesh and blood, but against the rulers, against the authorities, against the powers of this dark world....

EPHESIANS 6:12

CONTENTS

FOREWORD

By Ben Carson, M.D.

*A*ccording to Plan by my friend and respected economic forecaster, Kevin Freeman, is a clarion call to vigilance and action if we are to preserve America as "the land of the free and the home of the brave."

This nation was seen as an experiment by many observers in Europe and other parts of the world where people were accustomed to governance by a monarch or a ruling body. The thought of a nation ruled by the will of the people seemed farcical to many. Nevertheless, that model proved highly successful and has lasted for nearly 250 years.

The founders were diligent and studious. They carefully examined virtually every form of government and every major society that has a written history, acting as eclecticists by extracting and inculcating the elements of governance that lead to peace and prosperity while rejecting those things that ultimately lead to dominance and servitude with respect to the people.

America has weathered a plethora of obstacles, including a revolutionary war, a Civil War, two world wars, major civil unrest, and a host of other issues and not only survived but thrived. We now face the most formidable challenge to our system of government, as defined by our Constitution, that we have ever encountered.

Readers of this book will become familiar with the current iteration of forces that wish to fundamentally change our nation to something else. Resisting the Marxist tendencies of socialism will not only require courage and fortitude, but just as importantly, knowledge of the goals and tactics of our adversaries is essential. Like all evil forces, the promise of economic security "from the womb to the tomb" has served to seduce numerous societies over the centuries. Yet a careful retrospective analysis of those societies after Socialism has taken root demonstrates widespread misery and regret, except in the ruling classes.

As the author skillfully shows us, Marxist ideology cleverly presents itself early on as the gentle mechanism to achieve social justice. Creating a sense of victimhood and simultaneous entitlement stimulates the proliferation of widespread discontent, which facilitates the creation of an army of what many credit Vladimir Lenin as referring to as "useful idiots." These are frustrated people who can be manipulated into becoming the violent and threatening tools of power-hungry "pigs" as depicted in the book Animal Farm and ably employed as examples by the author of this book.

These people do not realize that they are working against their own interests. The mainstream media in America can also fit into this group since they are advocating for socialist principles without fully realizing that one of the first actions of Marxist governments is to fully control the media. Thus, they are actually working against the principles advocated by our first amendment to the Constitution; namely, freedom of the press.

Individuals like those wishing to alter the governance of our country have been ubiquitous throughout human history. And they have a lot to do with the latter of the eight stages of the rise and fall of civilizations. A number of eminent scholars have studied the triumph and the demise of prominent civilizations, and a consensus has emerged regarding the existence of the following eight stages of civilizations from:

1. bondage to spiritual growth
2. spiritual growth to great courage
3. courage to liberty
4. liberty to abundance
5. abundance to complacency
6. complacency to apathy
7. apathy to dependency
8. dependency back to bondage

We currently seem to be in the 5- to 6-stage, with many forces trying to facilitate the transition to stage 7. Remember dependents need a master or overseer. The power-hungry bureaucrats that are multiplying daily in America are anxious to assume that role.

This is America, and we are different. We do not have to inexorably move to stage seven and eight. In fact, this book can help us to reverse the cycle. We all have to be players if we are to win this fight. There is always a canary in the coal mine. Kevin Freeman may be such a canary. Will we listen?

—BENJAMIN S. CARSON, SR., M.D.

Founder and Chairman, American Cornerstone Institute, 17th Secretary, United States Department of Housing and Urban Development, Emeritus Professor of Neurosurgery, Johns Hopkins Medicine

INTRODUCTION

Seventy-five years ago, America stood tall. We defeated one totalitarian threat, Germany's National Socialists, and stood up to another, Russia's Soviet Socialists. We freed millions of people from tyranny, fed the world, and rebuilt the global economy. Here at home, families were strong, streets were safe, the job market was booming, and children learned timeless values at school and church.

Today, however, we see so many things going wrong.

Stores are looted, police defunded, and patriotism mocked. Schools are failing our children, replacing education with indoctrination. Crime, drug use, and suicide are all on the rise. Government debt and inflation are skyrocketing too, making the American Dream harder to reach for millions of families. Supplies are short, gas prices soar, and able-bodied men and women are paid not to work.

Meanwhile, our oil fields are closed but the border is wide open, destroying jobs and allowing millions to enter illegally. Our military is weakened by budget cuts, woke culture, and the discharge of unvaccinated soldiers. We retreat from enemies, leave weapons in the hands of extremists, have no answer for Ukraine or Taiwan, and are led by politicians whose families profit from America's foes.

And our deep commitment to community, once an American hallmark, is now fractured by woke cancel culture, critical race theory, and social justice discord. The fundamental freedoms of speech, assembly, and commerce are being restricted. Citizens are jailed, and a President's home is invaded for political reasons. And our right to choose how we live is denounced by so-called experts who impose rules they themselves disregard.

WHAT IS GOING ON??

Some say these crises are due to the incompetence or even insanity of our leaders. Others presume it's just a coincidence they are all occurring at the same time.

But I disagree. I took a hard look at all that's happening and came to a shocking conclusion: what we face today isn't the result of incompetence, insanity, or even coincidence. As this book will lay bare, these crises are happening *according to plan*.

Decades in the making, it is a plan to take down the greatest obstacle to totalitarianism the world has ever known: the United States. And it's a plan that *will* succeed—unless we unite and take action now to save America.

PART I

THE PIGS

I t's an unusual way to start a book, but I'm going to come right out and say it: *The "elites" are Pigs.*

I don't mean they are fat or fond of rolling around in mud, and they certainly aren't the source of delicious bacon. No, what I mean is the so-called elites are just like the pigs of *Animal Farm*.

In that bestselling book, George Orwell's pigs claimed to be for all. They led their fellow farm animals in a revolution, chasing off the drunk abusive farmer and taking over his farm. Initially, the pigs spoke of equality and even decreed that "all animals are equal." But it soon became obvious they thought they were better and should run the other animals' lives. In keeping with their self-appointed role, they gave themselves special luxuries and privileges no one else could have.

In other words, they really weren't for all—they were for themselves.

After assuming leadership of the farm, the pig Napoleon changed the decree to read, "All animals are equal, but some animals are more equal than others." And when a windmill collapsed, injuring and killing some of the animals, he didn't let the crisis go to waste. Declaring a state of emergency, Napoleon and the other pigs tightened restrictions on the farm animals and then moved into the farmer's house. There the pigs got fatter, dressed in clothes, and lived the high life, smoking, drinking, and playing cards while the other animals were forced to work harder, some even to death.

The pigs had become the very thing they'd sworn to destroy: *the authoritarian elite.*

George Orwell wrote *Animal Farm* in 1945 to warn the world about socialism. Not surprisingly, the book has been banned in many totalitarian countries. The reason is simple: the pigs who terrorized Animal Farm are a lot like the Pigs here and around the world who do all they can. For themselves.

Please know I don't say this lightly. In fact, I prayed on it because I'm mindful of what Paul says in Acts 23:5: "For it is written, 'Do not speak evil about the ruler of your people.'" But then I realized something very important. Our rulers *are* the people, and our officials are supposed to be the public's servants. And far too often these days, they are not.

Like Orwell's pigs, today's "elites" think they're better and smarter than the rest of us. They think they deserve to live better than everyone else. And they will stop at nothing to keep their good times going. They may talk a lot about equality (or "equity," to be fully current) but, in reality, their mission is what it's always been: to make themselves and their families as rich and powerful as possible, even if that means holding everyone else down.

THE PIGS TODAY

Need proof? A quick tour around the world should do the trick, starting with one of the biggest pig pens of them all.

COMMUNIST CHINA

In the "People's Republic" of China (that's what the leaders there call it, and with a straight face too), the Pigs run the show. The media may tell you China is Communist—a theory of government in which all citizens are supposed to be equal—but that's just for cover. In reality, power over China's 1.4 billion people is wielded by the "Paramount Leader" (I'm not making this up!). He runs a few *very* exclusive power structures with great names like the "National People's Congress" whose members are, of course, loyal not to the people but to him. Anyone who dares to dissent mysteriously goes missing or suffers an unfortunate accident.

From their political thrones, China's Pigs control daily life to an extreme degree. Want to live wherever and do whatever you want? Too bad. Infected with Wuhan's most famous export, the COVID-19 virus? Get ready to be locked down with barely any food. Want to practice Islam or Falun Gong? Sorry, our misguided friends—it's labor camps, mass rape, and forced organ harvesting for you. Dare to express concern about any of this? Your "social credit score" just took a hit, making it harder for you to work, travel, send your kids to school, and avoid public shaming.

Uyghur detention camp. GREG BAKER/AFP via Getty Images.

And the men who hold all this power (yes, ladies, the "People's Republic" is largely run by guys) are crazy rich, too. Mao Zedong, who led the Communist Party and ruled China for decades, dressed like a commoner—but his life was anything but common. According to China's own data, the average person ate 1,500 calories per day and had just a half a pound of meat per month. An estimated 30 million Chinese men, women, and children starved to death, but Mao stayed nice and plump on lavish meals made with delicacies flown in from all over the world. During his cruel reign, many families lived with three generations in a single room dwelling. Not so for Chairman Mao, who had more than 50 luxurious estates where he lived like, well, a Pig. Dancing was outlawed in China, too, but Mao's mansions were an exception. A coterie of young girls was kept there to dance for Mao and satisfy his sexual urges.

In many ways, current Paramount Leader Xi Jinping is little better. His family is estimated to be worth more than a billion dollars, even though Xi has never officially collected anything but a government paycheck. Hmmm. As *The New York Times* and Bloomberg News discovered, this topic is taboo in China. Their journalists compiled a damning expose of top officials' fabulous wealth, leading the communist regime to nix their visa applications. And just minutes after Bloomberg posted its story online, it was blocked by Chinese censors. "For journalists working in China," the *New Yorker* reported, "there is no more sensitive subject than the wealth of the top leadership; it poses more potential problems than anything one could write about Tibet or Taiwan or human rights."

Like a lot of Pigs, Xi leverages his power to lift his family far above the people he's supposed to be serving. Conveniently, many of his relatives have ownership stakes in companies directly benefiting from government contracts.

Chinese President Xi Jinping and his wife lady Peng Liyuan. Lintao Zhang/Getty Images.

That cozy relationship nets them hundreds of millions of dollars, enabling them to live like royalty. One of Xi's nieces, for example, bought a villa in Hong Kong's most exclusive neighborhood, Repulse Bay, for nearly $20 million. More than 600 Chinese workers would have to pool their entire wages (and not eat) to afford her swanky home. And that's just one of multiple luxury properties owned by the top brass in China. Meanwhile, millions of Chinese families continue to live on less than $5.50 per day.

Yes, the so-called elites in China certainly are Pigs, but as we'll soon see, they're not the only ones.

THE SOVIET UNION AND RUSSIA

"Reliable stronghold of the people's happiness!" So went the State Anthem of the Soviet Union when it was adopted in 1944. Spanning 15 countries and more than 8.6 million square miles, the Soviet Union was created for the alleged purpose of eliminating the wealthy aristocracy and making all people equal. Nice spin job, that. In reality, the Soviet Union became yet another pigsty where the "elites" became rich and powerful while the people suffered. Soviet leaders and their families lived in luxurious apartments and country dachas, not the small units into which everyone else was crammed. The elites had access to cars, too, something few average citizens could ever afford, and special lanes were restricted solely to the leaders' limousines. Food was scarce for the typical family, but the Pigs were able to shop and order specialty items from markets that only served them. Their children went to elite schools, and the healthcare services they received were the best in the country. Meanwhile, 1-in-5 Soviet citizens struggled to survive on just 75 rubles a month. So much for the people's happiness.

The Soviet Union collapsed in 1991, but that brought little relief. Russian President Vladimir Putin (another government employee turned multi-billionaire) lives like a Pig while millions of his countrymen struggle to scrape by. Along with a network of his closest friends, he controls nearly all of Russia's industrial resources, including much of its highly lucrative oil and gas production. This has enabled Putin to amass a fortune worth an estimated $200 billion, making him one of the world's richest people. Among his many properties is an enormous mansion on the Black Sea valued at $1.4 billion that is roughly *300 times* larger than the average Russian's home. And among his planes and boats is *The Scheherazade*, a colossal yacht worth $700 million that, according to one of its builders, is encrusted with marble and gold. Meanwhile, an estimated 1-in-6 Russians is destitute, with 20 million living on just $154 per month.

Multi-million-dollar mega yacht Scheherazade, docked at the Tuscan port of Marina di Carrara, Tuscany. FEDERICO SCOPPA/ AFP via Getty Images.

NORTH KOREA

Obscene income inequality exists in the communist "people's paradise" of North Korea, too. Supreme Leader Kim Jong-un has taken the Pig analogy so literally that he once tipped the scales at over 300 pounds. Still obese today, he follows Chairman Mao's example and wears simple outfits when the cameras are rolling.

But don't be fooled—the United Nations reported he spends vast sums on high fashion and watches, as well as alcohol and electronics. He indulges himself in these luxuries at more than a dozen palaces, one of which is so large it has its own sports stadium in addition to swimming pools, waterslides, basketball courts, and other pigsty priorities. And when he feels the need to get out, he has thoroughbred horses, luxury cars, private jets, exotic yachts, an armored train, and a private island where he parties with his "Pleasure Brigade," a troop of long-legged young women plucked from their families to serve Kim's sexual needs.

The "Supreme Leader" can afford all this because he's robbed his countrymen blind. In fact, the UK's *Express* recently estimated his net worth at $5 billion. He may feel this is as it should be, since the North Korean government has long claimed the Kims have godlike powers. But while he

Kim Jong-un in Lang Son, Vietnam. Linh Pham/Getty Images.

gorges himself and lives in luxury, his people are suffering. More than half of all North Koreans live below the poverty line (think about that), millions of workers earn just $200 per month, and hundreds of thousands languish in brutal prison gulags where rape, beatings, and murder are common. Not surprisingly, malnutrition is a common threat facing North Koreans, with nearly half of all people experiencing food insecurity and 1-in-5 children suffering stunted growth due to insufficient food. "Paradise" indeed.

IRAN

Wait a second, you may be thinking, *what is Iran doing on this list? Isn't it an Islamic nation run by devout clerics?* Yes, indeed. But beneath their pious garb are some pretty big Pigs. Iran's hardline Shiite Muslims have ruled this oil-rich nation ever since deposing the Shah in 1979. In public, they appear as one would expect of a cleric, with turbans on their heads and cloaked in simple brown or black robes. From all appearances, they live the humble life they harshly impose on their subjects. Behind the scenes, however, they are every bit a match for their authoritarian allies.

An Iranian boy plays with mud in a poor neighborhood near Tehran. BEHROUZ MEHRI/ AFP via Getty Images.

Iran's Supreme Leader (here we go again) is a dour fellow named Ali Khamenei. Although he claims to live modestly, he really has no need to look so gloomy. After all, the U.S. State Department reports Khamenei is worth "$200 billion, while many people languish in poverty." Along with his family, he owns vast real estate holdings, commercial enterprises, and hundreds of millions of dollars' worth of gold and diamonds, putting them solidly in the 4% of Iran's population that controls the bulk of the nation's wealth. Meanwhile, an estimated 4-in-5 Iranians live below the poverty line, some in such desperate straits they must sell their organs for the money needed to feed their family.

CUBA

For years, experts studying the island nation just ninety miles off Florida's coast assumed Fidel Castro and his family were wealthy. After all, they led a so-called communist country, which as we've already seen are notorious for "elite" privilege amid dire poverty. It was not until Castro's longtime bodyguard, Juan Reinaldo Sanchez, escaped to America, however, that insider details of Castro's piggishness became public. Sanchez was in Castro's inner sanctum for seventeen years, giving him direct access to Cuba's "revolutionary" leader. What he revealed in his 2014 book, *The Hidden Life of Fidel Castro*, underscored the massive income inequality that all authoritarian regimes brazenly foster.

Castro lived in "luxury that most Cubans can't even imagine," said Sanchez, even though Fidel claimed to draw a salary of just $36 per month. Like his fellow Pigs around the world, Castro's lifestyle featured numerous properties, rich possessions, a fleet of luxury cars, a custom yacht, and much more. (Fittingly, Castro also had a private island in the Bay of Pigs.) The average Cuban earns less than $50 per month, has limited access to food and medicine,

and must maintain 65-year-old cars because they can't afford anything else. But their piggish leader and his family amassed a fortune estimated at more than $1 billion. No wonder thousands of Cubans took to the streets in July 2021 waving American flags and demanding an end to communism.

Fidel and Raul Castro. Antonio RIBEIRO/ Gamma-Rapho via Getty Images.

VENEZUELA

The final visit on our quick tour is to a place once hailed as the richest country in South America— before Hugo Chavez rose to power, that is. After trying to topple Venezuela's democratically elected government in a military coup, Chavez adopted the tone of a moderate and ran multiple times for president, finally succeeding in 1998. But then the moderation disappeared as he pursued a socialist agenda eerily similar to what America's Progressives call for today. In short order, he shredded Venezuela's Constitution in the name of "social justice." He packed the country's Supreme Court with twelve new members beholden to him. The Chavez government then censored free speech, confiscated private property, and took over thousands of businesses.

Today, the formerly wealthy nation is called a "basket case." Many Venezuelans earn just $1 per day, thirty percent of them

Nicolas Maduro, Venezuela's president, center, his wife Cilia Flores, left, and Gladys Gutierrez, president of the Venezuelan Supreme Court. Carlos Becerra/Bloomberg via Getty Images.

cannot find food for more than one meal a day, and families have resorted to eating rats, stray dogs, and zoo animals to keep from starving. Inflation roared to a high of 2,000,000 percent (not a typo), and babies face a high risk of death due to an infant mortality rate that is now 400 percent higher than America's. But for Chavez and his equally piggish successor, Nicolas Maduro, life is good. They 'mysteriously' became billionaires, as did their families. For example, Chavez's daughter, Maria, is Venezuela's richest woman, with an estimated net worth of $4.2 billion. And of course, they own luxurious mansions and ranches, and fly private jets around the world to enjoy their lavish lifestyle. While most Venezuelans can no longer afford meat, a 2018 photo went viral showing chubby Maduro and his equally well-fed wife gorging on high-priced delicacies at celebrity chef Salt Bae's restaurant in Turkey.

WORLD DOMINATION

As evil as the Pigs are in China, Russia, North Korea, Iran, Cuba, and Venezuela, they have their sights set on even bigger prey: the entire world. Along with their globalist comrades, they seek to gain hegemonic power via a "one-world" government—that they and their fellow globalists would run, of course. This invitation-only group actually believes all economic, political, military, and social power ought to belong to themselves, the enlightened few. They're convinced they are the only ones who should run the world and be rewarded with its spoils. And what about the rest of us? As Hilary Clinton said, we are mere "deplorables" who deserve little—and will get it.

Among these Pigs is George Soros, a Hungarian-born billionaire regarded as "the almighty leader of globalists." With a record that includes tax fraud and insider trading, Soros uses his vast wealth to undermine the nation he has called "the primary opponent of global institutions"—America. His animus to us runs so deep, in fact, he has stated, "The main obstacle to a stable and just world order is the United States." Soros bankrolls groups and candidates who share his twisted agenda of defunding police, releasing criminals, opening borders, eliminating Voter ID, and much more. A notable recipient of

Billionaire investor George Soros. Adam Berry/Bloomberg via Getty Images.

his money is Black Lives Matter, an organization led by self-admitted Marxists and linked to bloody street violence. The Ploughshares Fund, a key backer of Iran's quest for nuclear weapons, is another. Soros' wealth has also underwritten major media outlets, journalists, Media Matters, and National Public Radio, which on July 4, 2022 ended its longstanding tradition of reading the Declaration of Independence. And he's now financing the Marxist-leaning Latino Media Network's purchase (and censorship) of conservative radio stations in Hispanic communities. He bankrolls the election campaigns of woke prosecutors, including Chesa Boudin of San Francisco, whose parents were members of the Weather Underground terror group and who is so far left he once worked for Hugo Chavez. San Francisco voters wisely kicked Boudin out of office, but that hasn't stopped Soros from funneling tens of millions more to a rogues' gallery of political action committees and public officials who share Soros' desire to destabilize America.

Klaus Schwab, chairman of the World Economic Forum (WEF). Matthew Lloyd/Bloomberg via Getty Images.

German-born Klaus Schwab is another of these globalist Pigs. He's the founder of the infamous World Economic Forum (WEF), which regularly convenes the world's ruling class in Davos, Switzerland to audaciously plan *our* future. Schwab believes the world needs "entirely new foundations for our economic and social systems." Towards that end, he is a principal architect of the Great Reset. As exposed by Glenn Beck in his terrific book, the Great Reset is an elite-concocted scheme to replace free enterprise and citizen democracy with a monopolistic, autocratic system of corporate-socialism run by (you guessed it) Pigs like him. Among Schwab's top advisers is Yuval Noah Harari, who is well known for pondering what the elites should do with the majority of humankind who he calls "useless people." Schwab hasn't decried this sentiment, perhaps because it is right in line with his upbringing. Born in Ravensburg, Germany, where the nightmare of killing disabled "useless people" began, Schwab was the eldest child of Eugen Schwab, manager of the infamous Escher-Wyss Ravensburg plant that manufactured weapons for the Nazis as well as turbines the Nazis used to produce heavy water for their atomic bomb project. Designated a "National Socialist Model Company" by Adolf Hitler, the Schwab-run company made extensive use of WWII slave labor, including Allied POWs. Schwab's family has since married into China.

To give you a sense of what the globalists have in mind, consider their Great Reset plans for changing how the world engages in commerce and addresses public health. If they get their way, both of these insidious goals will fall under the centralized control of an enormous government bureaucracy led by an international cabal of elites who will be unaccountable to sovereign nations, including America.

In the case of commerce, the globalists want every nation to participate in a truly wacky idea called Modern Monetary Theory. Under MMT, countries would print as much money as they want, spend it on vast government projects, and not care a whit for deficits or debt. As we're already seeing under Biden, unfettered money printing and deficit spending produces high inflation, making the poor even poorer and destroying the value of currency.

But that's just fine with the globalists. Their ultimate goal is to replace individual national currencies—and especially the world's benchmark, the U.S. dollar—with one or more global digital currencies. Known as Central Bank Digital Currencies, CBDCs would weaken national sovereignty and give international elites unprecedented control over the world's commerce and communities. Don't believe me?

Agustin Carstens. Andrew Harrer/ Bloomberg via Getty Images.

Then consider what Augustin Carstens, General Manager of the Bank for International Settlements (essentially, the central bank of central banks) himself revealed. "With the CBDC, the central bank will have absolute control," Carstens said, "and also we will have the technology to enforce that."

It should come as no surprise China is a big supporter of all this. Chinese Communist Party members serve on the World Economic Forum's board, and China is developing a digital alternative to traditional currencies that would shift wealth and power to the elites. They've got plenty of company, including here in the United States. Federal Reserve Chairman Jerome Powell, for example, has called digital currency a "high priority project." President Biden issued an Executive Order in March 2022 elevating creation of a CBDC to "the highest urgency." And Securities and Exchange Commission Chairman Gary Gensler, along with his close ally Senator Elizabeth Warren, is working to clear the deck for CBDC by pushing for regulations that will stifle freely exchanged cryptocurrencies.

In similar fashion, globalist Pigs have developed so-called Environmental, Social, and Governance (ESG) standards against which they want all companies and investments to be graded. Any company failing to earn their affection—such as fossil fuel producers, gun manufacturers, and anyone not toeing their politically correct line—will get low scores. And, ultimately, those with low scores will lose access to banking services and the capital they need to operate. Devious, huh?

But that's not all. Schwab, Soros, and other Great Reset globalists also aim to subject every nation to an international compact governing pandemic prevention and response. Even though COVID-19 exposed how much public health experts *don't* know, the globalists want to empower them to establish controls that would apply to everyone. Don't think you need to wear a face mask forever? Too bad, you'll be made to do so if the international bigwigs decree it so. Object to being administered an untested vaccine? You'll have to roll up your sleeve anyway if the ruling class says you must. Such an abandonment of individual and national rights was once just the stuff of science fiction, but if the Global Resetters get their way, it will soon be fact.

If you're shaking your head at all this, join the club—I am too. But if your reaction is, *Thank God American lawmakers are different*…well, think again. Because many of our politicians are Pigs, as well, and many of them are all-in on the globalist agenda.

AMERICAN BACON

T he unavoidable fact is some of our "public servants" are the most privileged people in the U.S.

Take Nancy Pelosi, for example. As a member of Congress for the past thirty-five years, she has earned a respectable government salary. And yet, she somehow managed to become filthy rich. How? She and her husband, Paul, have gone hog wild on insider trading, using her privileged access to market-moving information to accumulate a fortune that some estimate to be more than $200 million. They are also major investors in China, which must surely have been on the Speaker's mind as she blocked Congressional investigations into COVID-19's origins. The district Nancy supposedly serves is in full meltdown, with homeless families

Nancy Pelosi, with her husband Paul.
YURI GRIPAS/AFP via Getty Images.

living among feces, narcotics, and rats. But that didn't stop the Pelosis from buying a big-bucks Napa Valley estate, which is just one of numerous properties in her real estate portfolio, or from showing off multiple $24,000 SubZero freezers stuffed with $12-a-pint ice cream. Not wanting the good times to end, Nancy is running for reelection in 2022, reportedly so she can then retire and hand her seat over to her daughter, Christine. (Since when did America have hereditary succession?)

The Obamas are worth a look, too. When they moved into the White House in January 2009, Barack and Michelle Obama had a net worth of $1.3 million. Today, their wealth is reportedly *one hundred* times larger, topping $135 million by some estimates. That kind of cash can buy a lot of luxury and, in the Obamas' case, it certainly has. Their holdings include a DC mansion with nine bedrooms, a twenty-nine acre spread on exclusive Martha's Vineyard, and an oceanfront compound in Hawaii with two custom pools because, well, just because. The Obamas can afford all this thanks to a $65 million book advance and a $50 million movie deal along with book sales and speaking fees. But that's only half the story. The book advance was paid by a publishing company co-owned by Pearson, which received $350 million in taxpayer funds from Obama to develop the much-maligned Common Core initiative. And the movie deal is with Netflix, which pushed for and earned massive profits from Obama's net neutrality rules. Cozy.

US President Barack Obama.
JIM WATSON/AFP via Getty Images.

Or consider Joe Biden, who has been exposed as one of America's most corrupt Pigs by investigative author Peter Schweizer. In a series of jaw-dropping books, Schweizer reveals what the 'lamestream' media never bothered to report: Joe Biden's family—including his brother James and son Hunter— secured multi-million-dollar payoffs, corporate equity shares, and interest-free forgivable loans, thanks to Joe's influence and taxpayer-funded scams. Joe Biden famously claimed, "I have not taken a penny from any foreign source." But his family sure has—and, apparently, they then give a big chunk to "the big guy." How much? Well, as Hunter wrote to his daughter in 2019, "unlike Pop, I won't make you give me half your salary." That's scummy, to be sure, but what makes it downright dangerous is that tens of millions of dollars have flowed to the Biden family from China. One wonders what he's provided them in exchange.

There are many more Pigs in and around Washington these days, but Senator Dianne Feinstein (D-CA), Representative Eric

US Vice President Joe Biden and Chinese President Xi Jinping. PAUL J. RICHARDS/AFP via Getty Images.

Swalwell (D-CA), former House Speaker John Boehner (R-OH), and the Podesta brothers deserve special mention.

A senior member and former Chair of the Senate Select Committee on Intelligence, Feinstein has been a big China cheerleader, received illegal campaign contributions from China, and (oops) employed a Chinese spy on her staff. She glossed over the Tiananmen Square massacre where thousands were killed and invested millions alongside her husband, Richard Blum, in Chinese companies. One of them, Lenovo, then sold spyware computers to the U.S. military, giving China's intelligence agencies direct access to our defense forces.

Congressman Swalwell also has a thing for confidential information and Chinese spies. Thanks to an appointment by his pal Nancy Pelosi, Swalwell serves on the House Permanent Select Committee on (wait for it) Intelligence. Quite conveniently for Beijing, he also had a highly compromising sexual affair with a known Chinese spy, Fang Fang. Oh, and Swalwell's net worth has reportedly grown from pennies to millions while serving in Congress.

Meanwhile, John Boehner shows a Pig's time at the trough never ends. While Boehner served as House Speaker, the Senate passed a bipartisan bill to protect U.S. jobs from China's notorious practice of currency manipulation, artificially devaluing the yuan relative to the dollar. By making its products cheap here and ours expensive there, China deeply harms U.S. manufacturing. Naturally, China opposed this bill, so it hired the powerhouse lobbying firm Squire Patton Boggs to fight it. (Incredulously, the firm actually employs a member of China's National People's Congress, Nicholas Hiu Fung Chan.) Can you guess what happened? First, Boehner is said to have quashed the bill, preventing it from coming up for a vote. Then, when he retired from Congress, he was hired as a "senior strategic advisor" by (surprise!) Squire Patton Boggs where he continues to draw big paychecks.

But Boehner is by no means the only power broker pigging out in China's trough. Long a fixture in DC's lobbying world, Tony Podesta founded the Podesta Group which generated tens of millions of dollars in annual fees from clients that included a China-backed solar company. Conveniently, his contract coincided neatly with the work his younger brother, John, was doing at the very same time. Specifically, John Podesta served as Counselor to President Barack Obama, on whose behalf he was drafting the Paris Climate Accords. The outcome was virtually preordained: the agreement brutalized America's fossil fuel industry while treating mega-polluter China with kid gloves. It also called for a massive pivot to solar—a sector China largely controls thanks to its use of slave labor, below-cost prices, and a Biden executive order ending Trump-era tariffs that gave the U.S. solar industry a chance to survive.

Such are the ways of Washington, D.C. Because that city is such a big money maker for America's Pigs, many of them live as close to the Capitol cash machine as possible. Seventy-five years ago, manufacturing centers like Detroit, Baltimore, and Cleveland were wealthy for the simple reason they produced the most wealth. But as we'll discuss later in this book, many of those jobs were sent overseas, leaving unemployment and poverty in their place. Today, wealth is concentrated where the Pigs are—which is why the #1 wealthiest county in America is located just outside DC.

Sadly, piggish behavior is becoming more and more common among the political class. Consider the Scolds who instructed us to wear face masks and stay isolated while they had a great time (mask-free, of course) at Pigs-only events. President Obama's 60th birthday bash, California Governor Newsom's dinner with lobbyists, and Stacey Abrams' maskless visit to an elementary school all come to mind.

Consider too the Pigs who defund our police while surrounding themselves with special protection. Representatives Cori Bush and Ayanna Pressley are notable examples—they led the defund fight but spent thousands of taxpayer dollars on private security for themselves. Speaker Nancy Pelosi is another, having authorized the House of Representatives' Sergeant at Arms to fork over as much as $10,000 per lawmaker so they can install security equipment around their residences. She also deployed the taxpayer-funded National Guard to protect Congress from the people. (When it came to legislation protecting Supreme Court family members, however, Bush and Pressley voted no, and Pelosi chose to skip the vote altogether.) And ask yourself this: could anyone other than Hunter Biden be discovered with evidence of illegal drug use on their laptop and not be prosecuted? Or could anyone other than Al Sharpton skip paying taxes and yet avoid jail?

The fact is, when you take a close look at the politicians who are working hardest to build themselves up while keeping the American people down, you'll find lives of privilege, bank accounts stuffed with cash, special exemptions from the rules they impose on us, and a wide variety of measures designed to separate them from the "little people."

That's why I've written this book. The sad fact is there are Pigs in America, too. They've forgotten the Constitution begins with "We the People" not "We the Privileged." They ignore the fact our government is supposed to be "of the people, by the people, for the people"—not of, by, and for the Pigs. They've demonstrated they are available for hire, including by our enemies. And, like their fellow Pigs around the world, they've forgotten they are supposed to be public servants. That's why their actions are doing real damage to the nation we love.

This book will expose their plan. It will reveal how they've been putting it in action. And it will show what must be done to save America.

PART II

THEIR PLAN

with suppressing emotions." On the level of well-being, for example,
suppressed

Okay, you may be thinking, the Pigs sure are scumbags. But what does this have to do with a plan against America? The answer lies in our history and the principles upon which America was founded. Because who and what we are have made America the enemy of all who aspire to be Pigs.

Let's take a step back to our beginning. We speak of our nation's birth as revolutionary, and indeed it was—but not only because we revolted against Britain. To be sure, Great Britain was the most powerful nation on earth at that time, while we were mere pikers. But what made America's founding truly revolutionary was that we didn't replace one overlord with another. Contrary to custom, we cast off King George's autocratic rule and *didn't* replace him with a king of our own.

It's true some wanted George Washington to assume that mantle. After all, they worried, how could a nation be led if not by an all-powerful leader? But General Washington had other ideas. Having defeated the greatest army on earth and served his new nation as its first President, he wanted nothing more than to return to his wife, family, and farm.

This itself was revolutionary. As Thomas Jefferson put it, "The moderation and virtue of a single character probably prevented this Revolution from being closed, as most others have been, by a subversion of that liberty it was intended to establish." It even earned grudging respect from King George himself, who called Washington "the greatest man in the world" as a result. And it was made possible by the extraordinary vision of our Founders.

Rather than replace one authoritarian with another, they created an entirely new form of government. In the *Declaration of Independence*, they spelled out precisely how different it was going to be. "We hold these truths to be self-evident," they wrote, "that all men are created equal, that they are endowed by their Creator with certain unalienable Rights, that among these are Life, Liberty and the pursuit of Happiness."

Every American (or at least those educated prior to the destruction of our schools) knows these words by heart. And in our bones, we know what they mean: *the people* have the God-given rights to live, be free, and pursue that which will make them happy. In other words, America was founded for the specific purpose of protecting and advancing the smallest minority of all: the individual.

This was radical stuff at the time because, prior to America's founding, those rights were guaranteed solely to the elite. If you were royal or rich, life was pretty sweet. But if you were the son or daughter of a peasant, your life was preordained: you too would be a peasant.

Not in America. Here you could be anything you wanted to be, and many answered the call. Leaving dire poverty and dim prospects behind, millions came to our shores (legally) to pursue what soon became known the world over as the American Dream. A life free of tyrants, restraints, and anyone on high telling you what you could and couldn't say, do, or be.

But our Founders weren't done. The Declaration's next words are, "to secure these rights, Governments are instituted among Men, deriving their just powers from the consent of the governed." Where on earth were governments of, by, and for *the people*? Nowhere—until America's founding.

And thus was born American Exceptionalism. That term is often misinterpreted (including by Barack Obama) as suggesting America is better than other nations. Not so—it actually means America was created to be the *exception* to the rule that existed throughout the world before she came along. Here, power would rest not with the privileged but with the people. Determined not to repeat the age-old tragedy of tyranny, our Founders established a government that would serve the people by making its express purpose their liberty and happiness.

To be sure, the evil institution of slavery stood in horrific contrast to this vision, but here too America took an unprecedented path. From time immemorial, the crime of enslaving people has existed the world over. The Egyptians held slaves, as did the Romans, the Chinese, the Europeans, Native American tribes, and even Africans. Tragically, slavery still exists today. According to the Global Slavery Index, more than 40 million people are *currently* enslaved, most of whom are women and children. In fact, as you read this, they are laboring and being trafficked in Africa, China, Russia, India, North Korea, Iran, and more.

But the institution of slavery no longer exists here in America. Why? Because it was abolished more than 150 years ago after 360,000 Union soldiers and a President sacrificed their lives to end it. As Jason Whitlock puts it so well, they "made enormous sacrifices for their belief in equality and the freedom of other men who didn't look like them." This may sound odd to you. After all, you're being pummeled daily with the message America is inherently racist. Yet this very same America so embraced her birthright of freedom that she—unique among all nations on earth—fought a great war to ensure every one of her citizens would be free.

America also stood apart as a haven of religious tolerance. Settled by many who fled religious persecution in the Old World, America decreed in her Constitution that "Congress shall make no law respecting an establishment of religion, or prohibiting the free exercise thereof." As Thomas Jefferson explained, in America "the legislative powers of government reach actions only, and not opinions." For that reason, our nation saw the exuberant construction of churches, synagogues, mosques, and other houses of worship. And it's why Americans of all faiths live free of the imprisonment and executions that still threaten those languishing in fundamentalist and atheistic countries today.

America's unprecedented focus on freedom made some other wonderful things possible, too. Liberated from the chokehold of authoritarians, Americans were able to chart the course of their future, live where they wanted, learn what they wanted, say what they wanted, and make their fortune any way they could imagine. No wonder America became the world's engine of innovation. More inventions have been created here than in any other country. More Nobel prizes have been granted to Americans than to people of any other nationality. And more wealth has been generated here than anywhere else in the world.

Think about it: if you're reading this book on a computer, tablet, or smartphone, you can thank America for those devices, not to mention the internet and wifi they run on. If you prefer to read this in printed form at night, the electricity and light bulb making that possible were discovered here, too. And if you text or email someone about it...yes, that's right, those are also American innovations. In fact, so many lives have been changed and often saved by advances in science, manufacturing, medicine, agriculture, transportation, and more that were made possible by the freedom fostered right here in the United States.

Not bad for a nation that didn't even exist 250 years ago!

That's why America is the land of opportunity. A place where one's future is defined by one's efforts, not one's past. A place where the American Dream is available to all, not just the privileged few. A place where individual liberty is treasured and collective controls abhorred. A place where people don't fear their government—those in government fear being cast out by the people (as it *should* be).

But what's especially relevant to the focus of this book is the Founders didn't just make America the land of the free. Knowing *all* are created equal and endowed with the God-given rights of life, liberty, and the pursuit of happiness, the Founders sent a message to the rest of the world: these rights are universal and belong to everyone, everywhere.

The Declaration clearly states, "All men" (not just "all Americans") have been given these rights by God and are free to govern themselves within the rule of law. Government, the Founders decreed, should only do what the governed consent to. All else is reserved to those who properly hold the power: the people.

Put another way, no one—*no one*—has the right to rule or the destiny to be ruled.

This truth has echoed across time. Thomas Jefferson said, "Mankind has not been born with saddles on their backs, nor a favored few booted and spurred, ready to ride them." Abraham Lincoln agreed, saying this fact is "applicable to all men and all times." So did Ronald Reagan, who pointed out, "Our founding documents proclaim to the world that freedom is not the sole prerogative of a chosen few. It is the universal right of all God's children."

And that's exactly why the Pigs hate America.

As America grew in prominence and prosperity, she acted time and again to defend freedom from the evil of tyranny. After Europe was overrun by the National Socialists (Nazis) and Asia fell to the Empire of Japan, America entered World War II to lift them back to liberty. When the Soviet Socialists tried to crush West Berlin by erecting their infamous blockade, America airlifted nearly 2 million tons of food and fuel to preserve West Berliners' freedom. And when the Soviets brutally took control of eastern Europe, America sent the equivalent of $120 billion worth of aid to feed and rebuild the rest of Europe, helping it escape Soviet subjugation.

We also led the creation of NATO, the North Atlantic Treaty Organization, to be "a shield against aggression." The monumental importance of this shield was demonstrated yet again in 2022, when Russia invaded Ukraine—but didn't dare set foot inside a single NATO nation. In similar fashion, we have long defended South Koreans from their attackers in the north, protected Israelis from all who maniacally chant for their death, and stood with the Taiwanese in the face of China's repeated threats to retake what it falsely calls its "lost province."

Even when fighting for freedom requires putting our forces in harm's way, America is different. Throughout history, nations have used their armies to conquer, confiscate, and control. But not us—we free, we feed, and then we go home. As General Colin Powell put it, "The only land we ever asked for was enough land to bury our dead. That is the kind of nation we are."

Our efforts extend well beyond military action, too. In fact, America does more than any other nation to lift people out of poverty and support their quest for freedom. We provide more foreign aid than anyone else and work to help impoverished nations feed, house, educate, care for, and promote economic growth among their people. (By the way, the biggest beneficiaries of our support are in Africa, Latin America, and Asia, but don't tell the Left—it will complicate their "America is racist" slurs.) Little wonder the World Giving Index's 10th

General Colin Powell.
Bachrach/Getty Images.

anniversary report named America "the world's most generous country." Incidentally, China ranks dead last on that list.

Here's the key: as America grew in prominence and prosperity, tyrants recognized the threat she posed.

And no wonder. By lifting people out of poverty, America thwarts the tyrants' plans. When we fund and fight for freedom, we strengthen people's ability to resist tyranny and make them less susceptible to being subjugated. By doing that, America mucks up the works for those few who think it is their right to rule over the rest of us, dictate what we can and can't do or say, and enjoy lavish lives off the sweat of others.

That's why the Pigs have come for America.

By this, I don't mean Russian bombers are enroute, Chinese warships are shelling L.A., North Korea has launched its missiles, or Iranian-backed terrorists are committing more attacks. The tragedy of 9/11 will never be forgotten, but such acts can never bring us down. We know it—and they know it.

More specifically, they know Abraham Lincoln was right when he said:

> From whence shall we expect the approach of danger? Shall some trans-Atlantic military giant step the earth and crush us at a blow? Never. All the armies of Europe and Asia...could not by force take a drink from the Ohio River or make a track on the Blue Ridge in the trial of a thousand years. No, if destruction be our lot we must ourselves be its author and finisher.

So, they have been working quietly but relentlessly to take us down from within, to diminish America so she can no longer pose a threat to their tyranny. They've made a careful study of who our own Pigs and wannabe-autocrats are. They are methodically conspiring with and corrupting them. All for the purpose of weakening America economically, militarily, socially, and culturally.

Don't believe me? Well, then consider what the Pigs themselves have to say about their Plan to undermine America.

THE SOVIET UNION

L et's start with the Soviet Union (more formally known as the
Union of Soviet Socialist Republics, or USSR). Its founder
Vladimir Lenin reportedly
gave us our first warning: "We
will encircle the last bastion of
capitalism, the United States of
America. We will not need to
fight. It will fall as a ripe fruit
into our hands." To many, Lenin's
threat might have sounded like
mere bluster, but as you will see
in a moment, Soviet strategists
were in fact devising ways to
make it real.

Vladimir Ilich Lenin.
Bettmann/Getty Images.

His successor, Joseph Stalin,
doubled down on Lenin's threat. In fact, it has been reported
he said, "America is like a healthy body and its resistance is
threefold: its patriotism, its morality, and its spiritual life. If

Joseph Stalin. Bettmann/Getty Images.

you can undermine these three areas, America will collapse from within."

But Americans' love of country, decency, and God runs very, very deep. So, how did the Soviet Pigs think their plan could succeed? The answer lay in corrupting the corruptible: those U.S. activists and politicians who either sympathized with the brutality of socialism—or might be made to do so at the right price. With the complicity of these insiders, the Soviets realized they could make real headway.

Nikita Khrushchev ascended to the Soviet Union's top spot soon after Stalin's death and confirmed this strategy. "We will take America without firing a shot," he reportedly predicted. "We do not have to invade the U.S. We will destroy you from within." Khrushchev also provided a glimpse into the Soviets' plan. "We

Nikita Khrushchev. CORBIS/ Corbis via Getty Images.

cannot expect Americans to jump from capitalism to Communism," he said, "but we can assist their elected leaders in giving Americans doses of socialism until they suddenly awake to find out they have Communism."

Politicians are notoriously full of hot air, so it may be tempting to dismiss these

Soviet defector Arkady Shevchenko. Diana Walker/Getty Images.

statements. But we can't. Because what we've learned from key players who defected to the West not only confirms but also provides chilling details about the Soviet Union's plan to undermine America.

Consider Arkady Shevchenko, for example. A high-ranking Soviet diplomat, he served as a close advisor to Foreign Minister Andrei Gromyko and as Under-Secretary-General of the United Nations. This guy was *connected*, and his credentials were impeccable. In fact, his physician father even attended the Yalta Conference in 1945 for the purpose of spying on FDR's health.

Shevchenko enjoyed all the perks that come with being a pig. Serving in the Soviet ruling class, he said, means "you have all the privileges in the Soviet Union. You have huge apartments in Moscow with the servants. You have what they call Dutch country houses. You don't need to stay like the common ordinary Soviets in lines for food or something. You just receive every week a list of everything you want, and you pay even less than low price." (So much for the so-called "workers paradise," huh? In socialist regimes, only the elites live well.)

Despite these perks, Shevchenko sought to be free and defected to America. Once safely hidden, he pulled back the Kremlin's curtains and exposed that Soviets were indeed working with activists inside America to undermine our country. "There is a penetration of the pacifist movement by the Soviet agents," he confirmed. "They are very much effective in turning the pacifist movements, using the Communist Party in the west and trying to do the propaganda and everything, which is very useful for the Soviet Union."

Another Soviet defector, Yuri Bezmenov, had even more to say about propaganda and other aspects of the "Soviet subversion model." An agent of the KGB, the Soviet Union's notorious secret police, Bezmenov officially served as Deputy Chief of the Research and Counter-Propaganda Group in India before defecting to the United States. What he brought to light underscores how far our adversaries will go to undermine America.

As Bezmenov revealed, most of the KGB's focus is on "ideological subversion [and] psychological warfare. What it basically means is to change the perception of reality of every American [using] a great brainwashing process." Those of us whose kids have come home from school with anti-American materials, such as the 1619 Project and Critical Race Theory, will be painfully familiar with what Bezmenov said next. "Marxism-Leninism ideology is being pumped into the soft heads of at least three generations of American students without being challenged or counter-balanced by the basic values of American patriotism."

The danger posed by this insidious tactic cannot be overstated. Wherever it's been applied, you see, Marxism has separated society into two groups: the rulers and the ruled.

That's why it uses poisonous tools like critical theory to divide people who were or might otherwise become united. CRT is a classic example of this—as its name makes clear, Critical Race Theory makes everything about race. Its goal is to produce racial tribalism and gum up America's economic engine by replacing industriousness with entitlement, so it pushes the narrative that nonwhites are oppressed by whites. In America, where many peoples have long become one (hence, *E Pluribus Unum*) and opportunity is available to all, CRT was initially a tough sell. But by using schools to infect young minds with this poison, it is indeed threatening to accomplish its intended harm.

Bezmenov also shed light on what Shevchenko had cautioned was the infiltration of America's pacifist movement. "Most of the people who graduated in '60s, drop-outs or half-baked intellectuals, are now occupying the positions of power in the government, civil service, business, mass media, educational system." From that vantage point, they are taking action that destabilizes America in what Bezmenov called the "essentials: economy, foreign relations, defense systems." Anticipating the huge impact of "woke" leaders in our military and on Wall Street, Bezmenov said, "In such sensitive areas as defense and economy, the influence of Marxist-Leninist ideas in the United States is absolutely fantastic."

Bezmenov then warned us the next weapon used against America would be crisis. "It may take only up to six weeks to bring a country to the verge of crisis" leading to "a violent change of power structure and economy." (The restrictions imposed on speech, assembly, religion, travel, and commerce in the name of what we were told was a COVID-19 crisis may have been just the dress rehearsal.) The goal, Bezmenov revealed, is "to destabilize your economy, to eliminate the principle of free market competition, and to put a big brother government in Washington, D.C."

"The United States is in the state of war," he continued, "undeclared total war... You are not living at the time of peace. You are in a state of war, and you have precious little time to save yourself." In the hope of mobilizing action, he concluded, "The time bomb is ticking. With every second, the disaster is coming closer and closer. Unlike myself, you will have nowhere to defect to, unless you want to live in Antarctica with penguins. This is it. This is the last country of freedom and possibility."

Thanks to President Reagan's leadership, America outlasted the Soviet Union. But the Plan to take down America remains— and is accelerating.

COMMUNIST CHINA

Today, the plan's most dedicated practitioner is the Chinese Communist Party (CCP).

The CCP's aggression towards America began soon after it took over China in 1949. In the preceding years, the U.S. had fought there to end imperial Japan's brutal onslaught. Dr. Lianchao Han describes our role this way: "When the Chinese people and the Chinese nation were in peril, the United States came to the rescue and asked for nothing in return. The U.S. never occupied a single inch of Chinese territory, never reaped any particular reward." But to the CCP, any force for freedom is the enemy.

Founded by CCP leader Mao Zedong, the People's Republic of China has seen firsthand the horror of totalitarian control: it's estimated as many as *80 million* Chinese died during Mao's rule from 1949-1976. Mao himself said, "Communism is not love. Communism is a hammer which we use to crush the enemy." Nor was Mao's cruelty limited to his own country. The Korean peninsula was devastated by the war he fomented there, and one-fifth of all Tibetans are said to have died after China invaded and annexed their homeland.

Given these facts, it would seem obvious the threat to mankind was Mao and the totalitarian regime he founded. Obvious to everyone but Mao, that is. Instead, in 1968 he exhorted,

Refugees during the famine in China. Topical Press Agency/Getty Images.

"People of the whole world, unite still more closely and launch a sustained and vigorous offensive against our common enemy, U.S. imperialism, and its accomplices!" Did you catch that? Mao killed tens of millions, but it's the U.S. that is the "common enemy" to the "people of the whole world." As Joe Biden might say, "Come on, man!" (if his relatives weren't so snuggled in bed with China, that is).

Mao was clearly a blood-soaked madman, but his CCP cronies don't think he was crazy. Instead, they've been working to implement his "sustained and vigorous offensive" against America ever since. Consider General Chi Haotian, who served in the People's Liberation Army from 1946 to 2003 and rose to the rank of General. Chi also served in multiple National Congresses, on the all-powerful Politburo, and as China's Defense Minister. In other words, Chi was and remains a hugely central figure in China, so we would be wise to heed his words.

While running China's Defense Ministry from 1993-2003, General Chi said the scary stuff out loud in a secret speech to CCP leaders. It's worth checking out the whole speech at https://jrnyquist.blog/ and other online sources, but here are some very telling excerpts.

Chinese Defense Minister General Chi Haotian. Matthew Fearn—PA Images/ PA Images via Getty Images.

Echoing Hitler and his fixation with *lebensraum*, Chi said China's "first issue" is "living space... The environment is severely polluted, especially that of soil, water, and air. Not only our ability to sustain and develop our race, but even its survival is gravely threatened, to a degree much greater than faced by Germany back then." He then cast a jealous eye towards the West:

Anybody who has been to Western countries knows that their living space is much better than ours. They have forests alongside the highways, while we hardly have any trees by our streets. Their sky is often blue with white clouds, while our sky is covered by a layer of dark haze.

Their tap water is clean enough for drinking, while even our ground water is so polluted that it can't be drunk without filtering. They have few people in the streets, and two or three people can occupy a small residential building; in contrast, our streets are always crawling with people, and several people have to share one room.

But coveting thy neighbor's country is one thing—living in it is another. So, how could China's "first issue" problem be resolved? Simple! Colonize the West. "To solve this problem," Chi explained, "we must lead the Chinese people outside of China." Assuring his audience the idea wasn't his alone, he added, "Comrade Mao Zedong said … we could lead the Chinese people outside of China, resolving the lack of living space in China."

He noted, however, that the idea posed thorny questions. "Would the United States allow us to go out to gain new living space? First, if the United States is firm in blocking us, it is hard for us to do anything significant to Taiwan, Vietnam, India, or even Japan, so how much more living space can we get? Very trivial! *Only countries like the United States, Canada and Australia have the vast land to serve our need for mass colonization.*" (emphasis added)

"Therefore," Chi continued, "solving the 'issue of America' is the key to solving all other issues. First, this makes it possible for us to have many people migrate there and even establish another China under the same leadership of the CCP. America was originally discovered by the ancestors of the yellow race, but Columbus gave credit to the white race. We the descendants of the Chinese nation are entitled to the possession of the land!" (Yes, that's an actual quote. And keep in mind, not only are these the words of one of China's highest-ranking military figures—ever—but China has never disputed or made Chi retract them.)

Reaching his crescendo, Chi exclaimed, "Solving the 'issue of America' is the mission assigned to the CCP members by history." In fact, "the relationship between China and the United States is one of life-and-death struggle… Only by using special means to 'clean up' America will we be able to lead the Chinese people there. This is the only choice left for us. This is not a matter of whether we are willing to do it or not."

But since he realized these are the words of war, he cautioned his CCP colleagues, "We must conceal our ultimate goals, hide our capabilities, and await the opportunity." Then he spoke of strategy:

> What kind of special means is there available for us to 'clean up America'? Conventional weapons such as fighters, cannons, missiles and battleships won't do; neither will highly destructive weapons such as nuclear weapons. We are not as foolish as to want to perish together with America by using nuclear weapons, despite the fact that we have been exclaiming that we will have the Taiwan issue resolved at whatever cost. Only by using non-destructive weapons that can kill many people will we be able to reserve America for ourselves.

What "non-destructive weapons" did he have in mind?

> There has been rapid development of modern biological technology, and new bio-weapons have been invented one after another. Of course, we have not been idle, in the past years we have seized the opportunity to master

weapons of this kind. We are capable of achieving our purpose of "cleaning up" America all of a sudden. When Comrade Xiaoping was still with us, the Party Central Committee had the perspicacity to make the right decision not to develop aircraft carrier groups and focus instead on developing lethal weapons that can eliminate mass populations of the enemy country. [The obscene 'research' being undertaken in the Wuhan Institute of Virology now makes sense.] Biological weapons are unprecedented in their ruthlessness, but if the Americans do not die then the Chinese have to die. If the Chinese people are strapped to the present land, a total societal collapse is bound to take place.

Displaying what he probably mistakes for compassion, Chi then said:

From a humanitarian perspective, we should issue a warning to the American people and persuade them to leave America and leave the land they have lived in to the Chinese people. Or at least they should leave half of the United States to be China's colony, because America was first discovered by the Chinese. But would this work? If this strategy does not work, then there is only one choice left to us. That is, use decisive means to "clean up" America and reserve America for our use in a moment. Our historical experience has proven that as long as we make it happen, nobody in the world can do anything about us. Furthermore, if the United States as the leader is gone, then other enemies have to surrender to us.

There is much more in Defense Minister Chi Haotian's speech that is worth reading and carefully considering. It's also important to bear in mind he's never apologized for these evil statements, and the Chinese government has yet to denounce them. That's because China and one of its most senior military leaders believe, "It is indeed brutal to kill one or two hundred million Americans. But that is the only path that will secure a Chinese century in which the CCP leads the world."

So much for Joe Biden's famously casual take on China: "They're not bad folks, folks. But guess what? They're not competition for us." In fact, Mr. Biden, America's competitor and conqueror is exactly what Communist China wants to be.

Around the time of General Chi's secret speech, a disturbing book was published in 1999 by two senior colonels in China's air force, Qiao Liang and Wang Xiangsui. Entitled *Unrestricted Warfare*, its English translation was produced with a subtitle that left little to doubt: "China's Master Plan to Destroy America." In it, Qiao and Wang made a strategic case for undermining America through a "composite force" of "alternative methods of attack" including political, economic, network, and terrorist action. Their work was praised in official CCP publications, no doubt because the authors confidently predicted such a "grand warfare method" could unleash on America "the same and even greater destructive force than military warfare."

Towards that end, China began taking steps in the 1990s to bulk up its economic strength by shedding trade restrictions imposed due to its awful human rights record. Fortunately for them, Bill Clinton was more than happy to oblige. When he campaigned for the Presidency in 1992, Clinton pledged not to extend trade privileges to China, saying it would be an act of "coddling criminals." Just two years later, though, he gave it

Most Favored Nation status. Many were appalled, but Clinton's surprise move clearly had its fans, too, because when he ran for reelection in 1996, millions of dollars were illegally funneled to his campaign by highly-placed Chinese citizens. Called "Chinagate," this scandal soon made headlines, but Clinton kept selling America out, signing the China Trade Act in 2000 to pave the way for China to join the World Trade Organization.

Not long after, a colonel in the People's Liberation Army named Liu Mingfu authored *The China Dream*, which has become a perennial best-seller in China and is reportedly a personal favorite of Premier Xi Jinping. In his book, Liu presents a vision of China not solely matching the U.S. but eclipsing us. "The world is too important to be left to America," he writes. "China's grand goal in the 21st century is to become the world's No. 1 power."

Like *Unrestricted Warfare*, *The China Dream* focuses on a combined strategy for achieving global control. "In the 21st century, the construction of a powerful China is not only to build China into a market power, but also to make China a military power." China's military, Liu continued, "must be an effective force in the Taiwan Strait to counter U.S. military intervention, which would deter the United States from supporting Taiwanese independence with force." In fact, "China's military strength has to be more powerful than any rivals in the world to the degree and level that no nation can contain China's rise. No country shall set a ceiling for China's power."

According to leading experts, China's military might already surpasses our own in a number of ways. Their navy has more ships, and their army more soldiers than America's—and they show absolutely no signs of slowing down. In fact, Navy Admiral John Aquilino, Commander of the U.S. Indo-Pacific Command, describes China's efforts as "the largest military buildup we've seen since World War II."

On the economic front, the CCP's "Made in China 2025" and "Plan 2049" efforts offer stark evidence China also aims to use market power to undermine America. In its National Program for Science and Technology Development, for example, China's State Council put it bluntly: one of China's guiding principles is "leapfrogging in priority fields"—a pursuit that's been aided by their theft of $600 billion in intellectual property from us every year as well as short-sighted technology transfers by us. Made in China 2025 is an aggressive strategy to give China an economic advantage in ten critical sectors: IT, advanced machinery and robotics, aerospace, shipbuilding, trains, electric vehicles, energy equipment, biopharma and medical devices, farm machinery, and new materials. In other words, all the manufacturing sectors a country would need to lead if it wants to control the world's economy. Towards that end, the CCP is investing billions in the government-linked companies leading this charge, giving them even more of an unfair advantage over their American competitors.

The Chinese Foreign Ministry insists the West is mistaking MIC 2025 for a "formal industrial policy" that would harm foreign competition. And yet, with senior CCP officials running the show, it's foolish to view MIC 2025 as anything else. The Mercator Institute for China Studies offers this assessment: "China wants to obtain control over the most profitable segments of global supply chains and production networks." The Congressional Research Service has reached a similar conclusion, writing "the transfer of U.S. technology, capabilities, and tools to China could undermine the competitiveness of U.S. firms over time."

Meanwhile, China aggressively pursues unequal trading terms that give it an unfair edge over American businesses. Elon Musk put the situation well in a series of 2018 tweets:

Elon Musk ✔ @elonmusk   5h
Replying to @realDonaldTrump
Do you think the US & China should have equal & fair rules for cars? Meaning, same import duties, ownership constraints & other factors.

Elon Musk ✔ @elonmusk   5h
Replying to @elonmusk @realDonaldTrump
For example, an American car going to China pays 25% import duty, but a Chinese car coming to the US only pays 2.5%, a tenfold difference

President Trump believed this was wrong, too, and he took action to stop it. To pressure China to negotiate a fair trade deal with America, he doubled tariffs on Chinese imports and encouraged American consumers to buy products made in the USA. As you might expect, the Chinese Communists went berserk. Their official newspaper, the *People's Daily*, printed a piece warning that China would fight for "its legitimate rights and interests"—to hike up the cost of U.S. products in China, presumably. They called President Trump's action a "trade war." And then they ratcheted the rhetoric up still further by declaring a "people's war" on the United States.

You were saying, Mr. Biden?

As for when China aims to be number one, that's clear: 2049, to be precise. That year marks the 100th anniversary of Mao's founding of the People's Republic of China (hence, "Plan 2049"). By then, Premier Xi insists China will be the "global leader in terms of composite national strength and international influence." Already, China's total Gross Domestic Product (GDP) has skyrocketed from under $90 billion in 1980 to more than $12 trillion today—an unprecedented trajectory of economic growth.

Put another way, China aims to be the world's superpower, and it's doing everything it can to make it so…with a little help from its American friends.

with suppressing emotions.? On the level of well-being, for example, suppressed

TRAITORS IN OUR MIDST

Every superpower in history has had its enemies, those in other lands who sought to take them down. As a result, the sinister plans hatched by the Soviet Union and China should really come as no surprise, nor should the saber rattling from North Korea, the flag burning in Islamic strongholds, or even the sniping from Cuba and Venezuela.

Consistent with President Lincoln's prediction, however, America's enemies aren't sweeping into the U.S. like the Mongols into Eastern Europe (or Russia into Ukraine). They've long known any such invasion would be doomed because millions of Americans are armed and willing to fight for the country they love. As a result, our enemies have been working to weaken America's military, economic, social, and cultural strength from within. And as we'll see in a moment, they're doing it with home-grown conspirators and the political party those conspirators have hijacked.

First, however, a short civics review.

Surveys of U.S. Presidents routinely rank John F. Kennedy as the most popular Democrat to ever occupy the Oval Office. A

US President John F. Kennedy. Arnold Sachs/Archive Photos/Getty Images.

young, handsome World War II hero, JFK brought elegance and excitement to Washington, D.C. His calls to greatness captured the imagination of millions of Americans, and his tragic death evokes deep sorrow to this day. It's no wonder, then, that JFK retrospectives continue to appear on TV, in bookstores, and at grocery store checkout lines. Given his sustained popularity, it's also no surprise the Democratic Party frequently references him in its messaging.

But, as former Senator Lloyd Bentsen might quip, today's Democrats are no Jack Kennedys.

When JFK ran for President in 1960, he set forth an agenda that was right in line with his party's mainstream. As a result, it resonated with millions of Americans and propelled him into the Oval Office. But as we look at what JFK stood for, we're struck by how different the Democratic Party is today.

Consider defense policy, for a start. Kennedy saw military strength as the best guarantor of peace. As he put it, "Only when our arms are sufficient beyond doubt can we be certain beyond doubt that they will never be employed." By contrast, today's Democrats support deep military budget cuts, "woke" policies that weaken our armed forces, and the compulsory discharge of any serviceman or woman who refuses to comply with their vaccine mandates.

Tax policy offers another sharp contrast. JFK was a champion of lower taxes, which he knew would spur economic growth.

With tax cuts, he explained, "Every taxpayer and his family will have more money left over for a new car, a new home, new conveniences, education and investment. Every businessman can keep a higher percentage of his profits in his cash register or put it to work expanding or improving his business." Today's Democrats are miles from there—they think taxes should be hiked whenever possible. In fact, Joe Biden has proposed the highest income tax rates in

Alexandria Ocasio-Cortez. Kevin Mazur/MG21/Getty Images For The Met Museum/Vogue.

the developed world, and his "Inflation Reduction Act" will take $304 billion *more* from the American people and eliminate 30,000 U.S. jobs, according to the Tax Foundation. Meanwhile, his fellow leftists unashamedly cheer for tax hikes, as AOC did on the expensive gown she wore to a $30,000 per ticket gala.

JFK differed on racial policy too, which he opposed as counterproductive. "I don't think quotas are a good idea," he said. "We are too mixed, this society of ours, to begin to divide ourselves on the basis of race or color." His view, of course, is sacrilegious among today's Democrats, who not only believe racial preferences are good but insist that "black lives matter" is right while "all lives matter" is racist—stances designed to divide Americans in exactly the way JFK denounced.

This comparison could continue, but let's conclude with two of today's hottest topics: abortion and gun rights. JFK was deeply passionate about the sanctity of life and called abortion "repugnant to all Americans." No surprise, then, that he nominated Byron White to the Supreme Court, who subsequently dissented from *Roe v. Wade*. JFK was also a lifetime member of the National Rifle Association and strongly believed in the Second Amendment. "We need a nation of minutemen," he said, "citizens who are not only prepared to take up arms, but citizens who regard the preservation of freedom as a basic purpose of their daily life, and who are willing to consciously work and sacrifice for that freedom."

If the Democrats' most popular President could somehow come back today, it's obvious he would have little in common with the party he once led. But the divide between Democrats past and their party today doesn't only relate to JFK—not by a long shot.

Take Barbara Jordan, for example. One of America's great

Barbara Jordan. Nancy R. Schiff/Getty Images.

civil rights leaders and the first black woman from the South to be elected to Congress, Jordan was honored by Bill Clinton with the Presidential Medal of Freedom. She was a lifelong Democrat who also was the first woman—of any race—to give the keynote address at a Democratic National Convention.

Among Congresswoman Jordan's many areas of expertise was immigration. Here, too, we see a huge difference between Democrats then and now. Jordan served as Chair of the U.S. Commission on Immigration Reform, where she took a strong stand against illegal entry into the U.S. "For our immigration policy to make sense," she said, "it is necessary to make distinctions between those who obey the law, and those who violate it." Tell that to today's "sanctuary city" types! Jordan also made a sharp distinction between who should be served by taxpayer-funded programs. "One thing is very clear," she said bluntly. "Illegal immigrants are not entitled to benefits."

Today's Democratic Party is on what you might call a *very* un-Jordan path. Far-Left Democrats have flung open our southern border to anyone who wants to cross it and are resettling illegals all over the U.S. They're spending billions on benefits and paying for lawyers so our legal system can be used to help illegals skirt our nation's laws. And as will be discussed later in this book, Democrats are even pushing for legislation that would allow illegals to vote in our elections!

How did such a divide occur? The answer lies in the decades following JFK's assassination and Jordan's retirement from Congress.

AMERICAN RADICALS

nitially, communists and socialists dwelled in the dark corners of American society. A more visible presence began, however, with the formation of the Socialist Party of America (SPA) in 1901 and the Communist Party USA (CPUSA) in 1919. Neither attracted many members, but their impact was boosted when the Soviet Union started to infiltrate Washington, including its most significant power centers.

Beginning in the 1920s, Soviet intelligence actively recruited sympathetic Americans to spy on the U.S. In the years that followed, their plan against our nation became known. In 1932, William Z. Foster wrote *Toward Soviet America*, a detailed manifesto promoting Communism to "the oppressed and exploited masses of workers and poor farmers." In it, Foster laid out the Communist vision for a revolution by those who he and other Communist leaders hoped would "cut their way out of the capitalist jungle to Socialism." Born in Massachusetts, Foster was a radical labor organizer who joined the Socialist and Communist parties, rising to serve as CPUSA's General Secretary from 1945-1957. (Fittingly for such a traitor, he breathed his last while in Moscow and was given a state funeral in Red Square with Nikita Khrushchev himself leading the burial procession.)

The 1950s also saw CPUSA's formulation of its 45 Goals for America. Chillingly detailed in W. Cleon Skousen's landmark work, *The Naked Communist*, these goals were read into the Congressional Record in 1963 so they could never be hidden. (I knew Dr. Skousen and traveled with him in the 1970s, accompanying my father who was on the board of his Freemen Institute.) All forty-five can be found at http://www.ecjones.org/1963_Communist_Goals.pdf and are worth reviewing because many, like these excerpts, are disturbingly familiar to Americans today:

#17. Get control of the schools. Use them as a transmission belt for socialism and current Communist propaganda. Soften the curriculum. Get control of teachers' associations. Put the party line in textbooks.

#20. Infiltrate the press. Get control of book-review assignments, editorial writing, policymaking positions.

#21. Gain control of key positions in radio, TV, and motion pictures.

#25. Break down cultural standards of morality by promoting pornography and obscenity in books, magazines, motion pictures, radio, and TV.

#28. Eliminate prayer or any phase of religious
expression in the schools on the ground that it
violates the principle of "separation of church
and state."

#37. Infiltrate and get control of big business.

#40. Discredit the family as an institution. Encourage
promiscuity and easy divorce.

This is what communists and socialists have been working to do to America. The list goes on, with directives that include undermining American institutions, discrediting the Constitution and our Founding Fathers, and more. But the goal that relates most closely to the Democratic Party's radical shift since JFK and Jordan is this:

#45. Capture one or both of the political parties in
the United States.

Because, you see, that's exactly what they've done.

Early on, American communists and socialists set their sights on the Democratic Party. Defining their agenda as "anti-anti-communism" (which is to say, anti-American), they forged what became known as the New Left, a political movement that hated America and was determined to fundamentally "transform" it. But doing so would require them to move from the periphery to power. How? The Democratic Socialists of America (DSA) website provides the answer: America's radicals set their focus on "Bringing Socialism from the Margins to the Mainstream." And their path lay in taking over the Democratic Party.

To its credit, the party tried to resist. The 1968 Democratic National Convention in Chicago is a case in point. Gathering to nominate a Presidential nominee, Democrats encountered 10,000 hippie protestors led by the cynically named Students for a Democratic Society (SDS). Consistent with their Soviet and Chinese mentors, the protestors opposed the Vietnam War and, thus, the Democrats' leading candidate, Hubert Humphrey, who backed continued involvement in Vietnam.

Demonstrators attack Chicago Police. Bettmann/Getty Images.

The result was a week of unrest spanning August 22-29, 1968 and culminating in "The Battle for Michigan Avenue," an all-out riot that saw 100 protestors and 119 police officers injured .

Humphrey left Chicago with the nomination, only to be bested by Richard Nixon that November. But the Left was now on a roll. To up their game, they founded the DSA in 1971 with the merger of two rather sketchy organizations, the Democratic Socialist Organizing Committee (DSOC) and the New American Movement (NAM). DSOC was a network of unionists, leftists, and civil rights activists who infiltrated a "New Politics" coalition within the Democratic Party's liberal George McGovern wing. Meanwhile, NAM was comprised of radical 1960s students, including the notorious SDS, and was dedicated to "revolutionary democratic socialist-feminist" grassroots action. In other words, DSA became a mixing bowl of the most virulent communist and socialist elements in America.

By 1972, the DSA's influence within the Democratic Party had gained real strength, and they succeeded in getting their anti-war candidate, McGovern, named the Democratic nominee. He fared far worse than Humphrey, getting shellacked by Nixon 49 states to 1 and revealing how out of step the radicals were with mainstream America. But in the bigger picture, the Left won: many of the radicals McGovern attracted to his campaign stayed inside the Democratic Party. And proceeded to move it far from JFK and Jordan.

We should note this act of political jujitsu was entirely in keeping with the Left's master strategist in the U.S., the infamous community organizer Saul Alinsky. Alinsky, who personally mentored Hilary Clinton and was a role model for Barack Obama, urged his followers to attain power by penetrating major institutions and then, once inside, commandeering them. "True revolutionaries do not flaunt their radicalism," he told them. "They cut their hair, put on suits and infiltrate the system from within."

Many Americans fled the Democratic Party as this got underway, including Ronald Reagan who'd been a member for much of his life. "I didn't leave the Democratic Party," he observed. "The party left me." And many are fleeing still, like Elon Musk who announced in 2022 he could no longer support what he called "the party of division and hate." (Not coincidentally, the once-adoring Left turned on Musk the moment he made this announcement.)

Meanwhile, those who stayed have made it their mission to cement the change articulated by goal #15: capturing a major

U.S. political party. These DSA types—including communists, socialists, Marxists, and other violent radicals of the 1960s and 1970s—hijacked the Democratic Party and changed its agenda dramatically. Centrist Democrats at the federal, state, and local levels were swept aside. Instead, key posts went to activists whose priorities bore no resemblance to JFK and Jordan's. And all of this gave rise to Far-Left DINOs (Democrats in Name Only), a collection of misfits that includes many of the politicians we see in Washington today.

> **DINO** /dī-nO/ *noun*, An individual who claims to be a Democrat but is actually a Communist, Socialist, or other Leftist."

This is why today's Democratic Party does so many things JFK and Jordan would have opposed. As we'll explore in Part III, DINOs forced small businesses to close during the pandemic but kept big-box stores open. They executed trade deals that shattered industrial America and sent our jobs to China. They consistently side with Big Tech instead of its users and with Wall Street instead of pensioners. And they shut down U.S. energy, destroying jobs and forcing Americans to pay huge sums to foreign oil producers. Like their fellow elites worldwide, you see, America's authoritarians side with the powerful instead of with the people.

How complete is DINOs' capture of what many Americans fondly recall as the Democratic Party? According to the radicals themselves, it's as complete as complete can be. Huge sums now flow to party leftists from George Soros and like-minded billionaire elites in Hollywood, Silicon Valley, and Wall Street. Far-left ideology is also propagandized in Democratic packaging across college campuses and public schools by violent agitators like Antifa and Black Lives Matter, by the American Federation of Teachers and the pro-China propaganda machine known as NewsGuard, and in the semantically tortured name of environmental and social justice. Communist Party USA leaders have spoken of their efforts "to capture the Democratic Party *entirely*." (emphasis added) And MoveOn.org's Political Action Director, Eli Pariser, nailed it when he said, "it's our party: we bought it, we own it"—indeed.

For all that, you may have never heard the term "DINO" before. That's because, when their takeover of the Democratic Party was done, Leftists began calling themselves by a name they think sounds better but which, in reality, far more revealingly aligns with their radical agenda than "Democrat":

"Progressive"

Today, sadly, the Democratic Party is little more than a front group for the progressive Far Left. In fact, more than 1-in-3 of all Democrats in Congress are currently members of the Congressional Progressive Caucus, many of whom are now or were at one time officially affiliated with communists and socialists. And, like former White House press secretary

Jen Psaki. libertynation.com.

Jen Psaki, who has yet to apologize for wearing a hat bearing the symbol of murderous Marxist regimes, the bias of these radicals is increasingly on full display.

Indeed, many of today's Democratic Party power brokers were themselves active in the unrest of the 1960s and 1970s. (This is what Bezmenov was warning us about when he spoke of "people who graduated in '60s, drop outs or half-baked intellectuals ... occupying the positions of power in the government.") Just as troubling, their seniority and often-hidden backgrounds demonstrate how much they've corroded the Democratic Party. For example:

Nancy Pelosi.
Samuel Corum/
Getty Images.

NANCY PELOSI serves as Speaker of the House of Representatives, where she has reportedly amassed a $200+ million fortune from stock trades that would make any Pig proud and her husband's deals with China. She's also been supported by the Democratic Socialists of America and its Political Action Committee.

CHUCK SCHUMER, the Senate Majority Leader, is said to have a similarly close association with the radical Left. A Communist Party USA affiliate reportedly helped elect him to the Senate in 1998, and groups like the Working Families Party generate massive votes to keep him there.

Charles Schumer.
Andrew Burton/
Getty Images.

Maxine Waters.
Chip Somodevilla/
Getty Images.

MAXINE WATERS, another senior DINO in Congress, has long been tied to Communist Party USA-affiliated groups and the DSA's American Solidarity Movement. She's reportedly even hired people from the DSA and the pro-China League of Revolutionary Struggle to serve on her official staff.

BERNIE SANDERS, Vermont Senator and Presidential candidate, deserves my grudging respect for honesty: unlike his colleagues, he's open about his radicalism. He ran for Congress as a Socialist, pushes an all-out socialist agenda, was married in Moscow, and is proud to have DSA's strong support.

Bernie Sanders. berniesanders.com via Getty Images.

Jerry Nadler. Drew Angerer/ Getty Images.

JERRY NADLER chairs the House Judiciary Committee and led the Trump impeachment trials. He is said to have joined the Democratic Socialist Organizing Committee and the DSA, and he pressed Bill Clinton to commute the sentence of Sarah Rosenberg, a radical Leftist who—get this—helped *bomb* the Capitol in 1983.

BARBARA LEE has been in Congress nearly a quarter century and reportedly has extensive ties to the Communist Party USA. In fact, it's said she was a key member of its Committees of Correspondence. She also has made numerous trips to communist Cuba, and even boasts about "Comrade Fidel" on her Congressional website!

Barbara Lee. Bastiaan Slabbers/NurPhoto via Getty Images.

Adam Schiff. Jahi Chikwendiu/The Washington Post via Getty Images.

ADAM SCHIFF gained national attention for his role in the Trump impeachment trials and the January 6 Commission. Less well known are the rumors the DSA helped him win his first election to Congress and that he's closely tied to the Communist China-connected Committee of 100.

Ilhan Omar and Pramila Jayapal.
Joshua Roberts/Getty Images.

Nor are these senior DINOs the only ones steering the Democratic Party far to the left. Their younger colleagues—including **ALEXANDRIA OCASIO-CORTEZ, RASHIDA TLAIB, CORI BUSH, AND JAMAAL BOWMAN**—are even more brazen about their true affiliation: as of this writing, they are *officially members* of Democratic Socialists of America, which also strongly supports **PRAMILA JAYAPAL** and **ILHAN OMAR**.

KAMALA HARRIS seems to be equally as brazen. Raised by a Marxist professor, Harris is so Far-Left the nonpartisan GovTrack.us ranked her 2019's most leftwing Senator (yes, even more leftist than Bernie). As Vice President, she actually met with Communists in the White House to discuss labor activities.

Vice President Kamala Harris. Kent Nishimura / Los Angeles Times via Getty Images.

And of course, I mustn't neglect **BARACK OBAMA**, who served as the 44th President and reportedly remains *deeply* involved in White House affairs from his mansion just two miles away. President Obama's parents were known as communist sympathizers, and he was mentored by Communist Party USA member Frank

Marshall Davis. Obama also reportedly joined the radical socialist New Party in the 1990s because he thought the Democratic Party was too moderate, and he was actively supported in his campaigns by CPUSA activists.

President Barack Obama. Neilson Barnard/Getty Images for SXSW.

There are a lot of Far-Left radicals masquerading as Democrats at the state and local levels too, sadly, including **ROB BONTA**. While serving in the California Assembly, he introduced legislation allowing Communist Party members to occupy posts in state government. Bonta is no longer an Assemblyman, but don't breathe a sigh of

Rob Bonta. Liz Hafalia/The San Francisco Chronicle via Getty Images.

Angela Yvonne Davis, a self admitted communist. Bettmann/Getty Images.

relief. He now holds California's top law enforcement job, Attorney General, thanks to an appointment by his pal, Far-Left Governor **GAVIN NEWSOM**. Newsom's wife posted a video in March 2022 honoring Angela Davis, a Communist Party member who purchased guns used by inmates to take a judge and jurors hostage during their trial. (Mrs. Newsom doesn't seem to be concerned that the judge was murdered in the ensuing standoff.)

Nor should we leave out all those in senior legislative and administrative positions whose focus may be on riches even more than radicalism. Long overdue investigations are exposing widespread corruption among U.S. public officials. We now know many have received considerable sums from Chinese companies that have direct ties to China's military and intelligence agencies. Others are personally invested in them. And so, whether they're motivated by personal enrichment or fear of exposure (or both), these officials are taking action that benefits our adversaries—not America.

In fact, space doesn't allow me to expose all the DINOs now holed up in government positions, but you get the picture: the party once led by giants like John F. Kennedy and Barbara Jordan has been overtaken by the radical Left. As Democratic Congressman Kurt Schrader bluntly put it, "The socialist wing of the party is taking over." That's why the policies of the captured Democratic Party bear such strong resemblance to the 45 Communist Goals discussed above. In fact, if you compare those goals to what Far-Left Democrats are trying to accomplish now, it's really hard to tell them apart.

Because today's DINOs are fulfilling the plan laid out by America's enemies, foreign and domestic.

The leftists of the '60s and '70s are now government leaders, just as the Soviets intended. They have remade the Democratic Party into a socialist stronghold and, to Communist China's delight, are working to weaken America from within. Consider House Resolution 438, for example, which Barbara Lee introduced in May 2021 along with dozens of her fellow DINOs. Among other things, this measure calls for deep cuts to the U.S. military and the Border Patrol, an end to immigration enforcement operations on our southern border, a wide array of fraud-prone changes to our election process, extensive welfare benefits for illegals, and economy-killing Green New Deal policies—all paid for with massive deficit spending.

Or consider the hypocritical tenets of the DINOs' radical agenda. They oppose Second Amendment rights, for instance, and claim the Supreme Court's recent concealed carry ruling will cost lives. But in the next breath, they attack the Supreme Court's *Dobbs* decision even though overturning *Roe* will *save* lives. DINOs also advocate for abortion and transgenderism on the basis of freedom, but they have no problem limiting our freedom to speak, own firearms, hold private property, or be protected from imprisonment without due process.

DINOs aren't merely interested in bad legislation or contradictory stances, though. As the COVID pandemic revealed, they are seeking to replace our free society with an authoritarian state. And they're building their fortress with full confidence that, like their comrades worldwide, they will end up mighty and monied—the Pigs in charge of the American farm.

Make no mistake: the Axis of Authoritarianism is real. The elites who comprise it know exactly what they're doing, and they are pursuing their goals with grim efficiency. It may seem like our leaders are clueless idiots, but closer inspection exposes something very different. I know newspapers and TV pundits describe what DINOs are doing as dumb and wonder about Biden's mental state. But as the next section will reveal, these people are not incompetent, they're not insane, and the multiple blows we've been taking are no coincidence.

Instead, all of this is unfolding According to Plan.

PART III

THEIR PLAN IN ACTION

As we look around today, we see so many problems that threaten America and her future. Considered individually, it's tempting to write each one off as just another dumb act by another dumb politician who simply doesn't get it.

But when these problems are examined as a whole, a diabolical pattern emerges:

The elites are working to weaken America so she can no longer impede their evil plans.

For eons, their strategy has been deceptively simple and brutally effective: establish control, squash dissent, reign with terror, and become filthy rich. It worked for pharaohs, kings, emperors, dictators, and other tyrants throughout history, and it continues to work today. That's why authoritarian hellholes like Russia, China, Iran, Cuba, Venezuela, and North Korea have decadent oligarchs amid dire poverty. The Pigs win by making the people lose.

Then came America. Here was a nation built on the foundation of universal freedom. Freedom not just for the elites but for all mankind.

And that's exactly why the Pigs are targeting America. They know our freedom empowers ordinary Americans to accomplish extraordinary things. They recognize the unprecedented economic, military, social, and cultural strength our freedom has made possible. And they see we've been willing to use that strength to defend freedom, both here and abroad.

So, this small group of self-serving elites has come to an evil realization: it's them or us. Either they make America too weak to preserve and promote freedom, or America will continue standing in the way, preventing them from achieving their dream of dominion over the entire world.

The following chapters will expose just some of the *many* things the Pigs are doing to weaken America economically, militarily, socially, and culturally. As you consider each, I urge you to ask yourself three important questions:

Is this incompetence?

Is it a coincidence?

Or is it happening According to Plan?

ATTACKING OUR ECONOMIC STRENGTH

"The weeds of socialism are better
than the crops of capitalism."

—MAO ZEDONG

A merica's freedoms produced the largest and most vibrant economy the world has ever seen. So great was this achievement, in fact, that it gave birth to The American Dream, the unprecedented opportunity for each generation of Americans to chart their own path, prosper, and build an even brighter future for their kids.

In other words, the exact opposite of what the Pigs, here and abroad, have planned for the little people.

If, as Lenin did, you want America to fall to socialism like a ripe fruit, her vine of economic strength must be weakened. Likewise, if you want to eclipse America in key markets and colonize her western states, as Chinese Communists say they do, her engine of economic strength must break down. Why? As Mark Levin explained in *American Marxism*, "when economic conditions have weakened, causing social conditions to do the same, the political system is…ripe for transformation."

No doubt, the lamestream media will read this and scream "conspiracy theory!" (their favorite term—except in instances of *actual* conspiracies, like the coverup of Hunter Biden's laptop). But it's not a theory if it's backed by evidence. And as we'll see in a moment, there's plenty of proof America's foreign enemies and domestic DINOs are pursuing an agenda so harmful to our economy that its destruction can be their only aim.

Let's start with Joe Biden's first day in office.

ENDING OUR ENERGY INDEPENDENCE

It's a given that nations can't be strong without energy. That's why world powers throughout history either tapped that energy (if they were blessed to have it within their borders) or raided their neighbors to get it. In America's case, our economic growth was powered by the discovery of Appalachian coal, Texas oil, nuclear energy, and more. These tremendous energy assets helped America achieve the world's highest standard of living and protected our nation from having no option but to buy energy from other, often unstable, producers.

So, let's pretend for a moment that you've just been elected President of the United States. Let's also assume this isn't your first rodeo and you have a lot of experience in public policy—say, as a Senator for thirty-six years and Vice President for eight. As a result, you've been around the block enough times to know:

- ✔ American energy fuels our economic strength.
- ✔ American energy enables our people to live better.
- ✔ American energy protects us from depending on other countries.

As President, will you maintain or even expand U.S. energy production? If your name is Joe Biden, the answer is clearly a resounding "NO."

During his campaign for the presidency, Biden was caught on tape telling a voter, "I guarantee you, I guarantee you, we are going to end fossil fuel." And as we soon learned, he meant it. Beginning on his *first day* in the Oval Office, Biden ordered a moratorium on the long-standing policy of leasing federal lands for domestic oil and gas production. He put back in place an Obama-era rule that raises costs on the U.S. energy industry. He proposed new taxes, fees, and regulations on American producers. He threatened an end to U.S. oil exports. He joined with his fellow DINOs in Congress to support banning banks from financing energy production. He closed nearly half of the National Petroleum Reserve to drilling and canceled a massive oil and gas lease that would have made more than one million acres available for energy development. And, of course, he killed the Keystone XL Pipeline to "save the planet"—even as he lifted U.S. sanctions on Russia's Nord Stream II pipeline to Europe.

So, what happened?

Before Biden took the oath of office, an estimated 7.5 Million Americans were working in the energy industry. Since he took these actions, many of them lost their jobs. At the same time, the price of the average gallon of gas skyrocketed from $2.38 under President Trump to above $5.00, with diesel fuel costing the nation's truckers even more. In addition to costing

Americans more, the radical shift away from reliable energy sources is downright dangerous. It puts communities at risk, as police departments exhaust their gasoline budget and are forced to handle 9-1-1 calls by phone. It poses the risk of depressed economic activity, further raising the specter of recession. And it threatens multiple states with brownouts and blackouts that could cause havoc, especially for the most vulnerable among us.

Faced with such obvious problems, the DINOs quickly pivoted to the blame game. Biden blamed gas prices on Russia's invasion of Ukraine, even though Federal Reserve Chairman Powell testified to Congress that "inflation was high before the war in Ukraine broke out." Similarly, Congressional socialists like Rep. Pramila Jayapal blamed American industry, as if energy producers created the restrictions that prevented them from pumping oil!

In every respect, our energy security has taken a serious hit from Biden's actions. Under President Trump, America achieved energy independence and became a net energy exporter for the first time since 1952. But due to the damage Biden has done, we once again have to go hat-in-hand to Russia, Venezuela, Iran, and Saudi Arabia for oil—despite having all the energy resources we need right here at home.

Biden's attack on American energy independence is inflicting great harm on our nation. As of this writing, America's GDP—a key indicator of our economic strength—fell dramatically in the first two quarters of 2022. According to his administration's own data, 46 of our 50 states saw their GDP decline sharply, with his energy shutdown causing the deepest losses nationwide. And as Biden's policies sent shockwaves across the economy, overall growth stalled to *zero* percent, according to the Federal Reserve.

At the same time, energy prices in the U.S. soared, making it harder for millions of Americans to power their homes, run their businesses, and fuel their cars. Truck drivers are being hit especially hard, as diesel fuel costs threaten to disrupt the nation's supply-chain. Higher energy costs are driving up fertilizer costs too, forcing many farmers to reduce production and giving rise to higher food prices and the harrowing risk of food shortages.

And yet, the DINOs now occupying the White House are undeterred. In fact, Biden's hand-picked chairman of the National Economic Council, Brian Deese, admitted on national news this is all being done to fulfill their radical agenda. After being pressed by CNN about the unaffordable gas prices hitting American families, he said "This is about the future of the Liberal World Order, and we have to stand firm." I kid you not.

Nor is Biden alone in doing this damage to America. Wokesters on Wall Street are aiding his efforts to end American fossil fuel production in the name of so-called ESG investing. Revealing where their loyalties lie, some Wall Street firms are sparing Chinese companies the same pressure now being placed on their American counterparts. That's right—even though Communist China is one of the worst polluters on the planet, brutally represses its people, and fosters a shocking degree of income inequality, they get a pass while American firms get pummeled.

Equally unacceptable, Washington is helping Wall Street invest your money into the very Chinese system that poses such a threat to our nation's future. As just one of many shameful examples, the Biden Administration quietly reversed President Trump's policy of ending American investment in the Chinese Military Industrial Complex. The CMIC, you see, has been using billions of our dollars to build the weapons it could use against us. In June 2022, however, Biden quietly issued new guidance clearing the way for Wall Street to continue sending our money to China for that dangerous purpose.

It's impossible not to be struck by the hypocrisy inherent in both of these examples. While America's energy sector is being shut down and DINOs are trying to strip us of our gun rights, China is free to continue polluting and is using our money to build some of the most lethal weapons on the planet. This is economic warfare, plain and simple, and it's inflicting upon America higher inflation, unaffordable gas, a shortage of basic necessities, and a rising risk of conflict with a heavily armed China. But don't worry about the Pigs. True, it now costs the American family more than $60 to fill up their gas tank for a trip to grandma's, but President Biden is doing just fine. In fact, his regular visits home to Delaware cost him, umm, *nothing*. Instead, American taxpayers have to cough up millions of dollars for every one of those trips back to his basement. That's because this little piggy requires Air Force One, Marine One, a convoy, and round-the-clock Secret Service protection so he can nap in his own bed.

No need to worry about the Pigs overseas, either. Vladimir Putin loves higher gas prices and America's renewed dependence on Russian oil. After all, it means more of our money is going to him—and helps finance his war on Ukraine. To be precise, as of this writing Russia has reaped more than $100 billion from fuel exports since it invaded Ukraine. Xi Jinping is doing just fine too, because Biden had the gall to ship nearly 6,000,000 barrels of oil from *our* Strategic Petroleum Reserves to China!

For similar reasons, Premier Xi loves the Paris Climate Accords too, that awful deal Obama signed. Negotiated by the elites, the accord shackles America's energy industry to, get this, "combat climate change," even though the U.S. environment is ranked as one of the cleanest in the industrialized world (you can look it up). At the same time, it flings the door wide open for what *The*

Telegraph calls "Beijing's dirtiest little secret," allowing China to add to its 1,000+ coal-fired power plants. China is already ranked one of the dirtiest industrialized countries in the world, emitting up to 400% more greenhouse gasses than we do, but the Paris agreement permits them to spew even more carbon dioxide into the atmosphere. President Trump wisely exited America from this trap, but Biden returned to it on his first day in office.

Of course, none of this should really take anyone by surprise. After all, Biden told us during a 2020 Presidential primary debate where he stood on American energy: "No more subsidies for the fossil fuel industry. No more drilling on federal lands. No more drilling including offshore. No ability for the oil industry to continue to drill. It *ends*." His predecessor, Barack Obama, made it clear to us too: "If somebody wants to build a coal-fired power plant, they can. It's just that it will bankrupt them." And Far-Left Attorney General Merrick

Chinese steel plant. Kevin Frayer/Getty Images.

Garland invented a new Office of Environmental Justice to sue U.S. energy companies for what he calls environmental crimes.

Nor is that the end of the story. Instead, all Senate Democrats voted to kill a common-sense proposal that would have relieved America of climate-related restrictions unless China complied with them, too. And the DINOs in Congress are pushing for a total energy drilling ban in America as part of their economy-wrecking Green New Deal.

Energy independence be damned.

DRIVING AMERICA TO BANKRUPTCY

"The best way to destroy the capitalist system is to debauch the currency."

So said Vladimir Lenin, and for good reason: he knew the United States would fail if our currency became corrupted. Lenin died in 1924, but had he been able to stick around for another ninety-eight years, he'd be proud of what DINOs have been doing to the U.S. dollar.

Simply put, Washington is creating money out of thin air to cover spending that's bankrupting America. As a result, every U.S. dollar is now worth less, so it takes more of our money to buy the goods and services we need. Under Biden, this inflationary spiral has reached levels not seen in more than forty years. As I write this, the inflation rate has soared above 9%, way up from just 1.4% when President Trump left office. What many now call "Bidenflation" is crushing the working poor and middle class, with rates up more than 100% across a range of basic necessities, including gasoline, food, and mortgages. Even discount stores like Dollar Tree had to raise their prices 25% to $1.25.

Another consequence of Bidenflation is the Federal Reserve has raised interest rates by 0.75%, with more increases anticipated. In addition to making life harder for American families and businesses, this hike also increases the cost of the interest we must pay on our debt. Estimated to total as much as a quarter trillion dollars per year, that increase is further impoverishing America. And the increased cost of this debt service has to be borrowed because the federal government is spending way more than it has, resulting in even more deficit spending, even more inflation, and an even greater risk of America being driven to bankruptcy.

All of this is doing exactly what Lenin hoped: it is debauching our currency. When Lenin met his Maker in 1924, U.S. federal government debt stood at $21.25 billion. Just a century later, it is *143,000%* larger. In fact, according to usdebtclock.org (a must-see site), federal government debt now tops $30 TRILLION and is rising fast. To put this obscene amount into perspective, if you went out on a shopping spree and spent $1,000,000 every single day using your credit card, it would take you *82,000 years* to rack up as much debt as the federal government has.

As bad as that is, it's just part of the story. In reality, America is being crushed by an even larger debt due to something called unfunded liabilities. You see, those wizards in Washington thought it would be just great to saddle our country with spending they had no way of paying for. In fact, Congress has incurred more than $82 trillion in Medicare costs, $30 trillion in prescription drug and other healthcare expenses, and nearly $16.5 trillion in Social Security debt—all of which haven't been funded. Totaling more than $128 trillion in *additional* federal government debt, these unfunded liabilities are so crushing, Boston University economics professor Laurence Kotlikoff said "The evidence is in front of our eyes that we're bankrupt. It's not bankrupt in the future. It's bankrupt right now."

By the way, you may have noticed I say "federal government debt" and not "national debt" like the lamestream media does. That's because America's families and businesses didn't create this crisis—Washington did. Federal lawmakers and officials ran up the largest government debt in world history because they don't do what the American people have to do every day: make sure they have enough scratch to cover their spending.

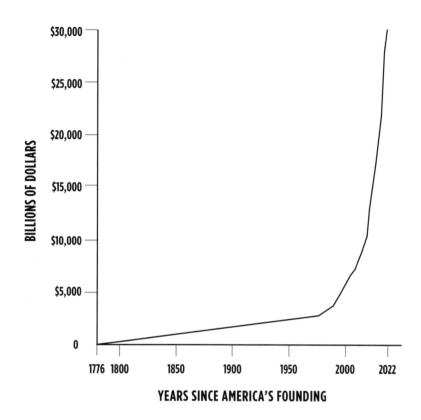

Instead, the federal government consistently spends more than it has. A lot more. For example, Washington spent $6.8 trillion in 2021, the first fiscal year of Biden's term. In and of itself, that's an enormous problem, but what makes it even worse is the government only had $4 trillion to spend. In just one year, it added another $2.8 trillion to the federal government's massive pile of debt. This led the Congressional Budget Office (CBO) to reveal a startling fact early in 2022: *just $4 billion* of the $1.7 trillion Biden spent on new legislation alone in 2021 was paid for. And he's only getting started—the Democrats' party-line passage of the cynically named "Inflation Reduction Act of 2022" will cause

Washington's ocean of red ink to expand even wider. If you were wondering why Federal Reserve Chairman Powell says, "The U.S. federal budget is on an unsustainable path", *this* is why.

Readers who are stubbornly optimistic may look at these numbers and assume (or at least hope) the money is being spent on good causes. If you're among them, forgive me for bursting your bubble. In March 2022, Washington's DINOs passed yet another government spending bill. Touted by House Speaker Nancy Pelosi as "historic," it ran to more than 5,000 pages of legislative text and related material. In fact, it was so long the Heritage Foundation estimated lawmakers would need nearly 400 hours to read it. Instead, they were given fewer than twelve. Why the rush? The official explanation was the bill had to be passed quickly because of its $13.6 billion in funding for embattled Ukraine. But the bill's total cost was $1.5 trillion, meaning for every $1 going to Ukraine, Washington spent more than $100 on other stuff.

Where, you might ask, did the rest of the money go? To DINO priorities hidden in more than 4,000 shameless giveaways called "earmarks." According to OpenTheBooks.com, the government's wasteful "pork" spending included $3.6 billion in stimulus checks—that were sent to dead people. As taxpayers, you also paid more than $2 million to teach sex education to prostitutes in Ethiopia and nearly $500,000 for a project overseen by Fauci's agency that injected hormones into male monkeys to make them female. And, of course, there's the $24 billion spent so federal government workers could have an average of 44 paid days off.

Congress even gave itself a raise of more than *twenty percent* for wages, trips, and other expenses of their offices. As a result, Congressional staff now make a minimum of $45,000 and can earn as much as $200,000. And as families struggle to find baby formula, their tax dollars are paying for a Congressional website where staffers can order beer, wine, and liquor to be delivered to their office! But somehow, Congress couldn't quite get around to banning their scummy practice of insider trading. I kid you not.

The damage being done by Biden and his fellow DINOs underscores how much the Left has changed the Democratic Party. Back in 1980, President Jimmy Carter rightly said, "Through fiscal discipline today, we can free up resources tomorrow." Long considered a big spending liberal, Carter nevertheless declared, "Our priority now is to balance the budget." How did the Left respond to Carter's fiscal responsibility? They tried to unseat him with a big-spending primary challenger.

But Biden is by no means the only Democrat to reject fiscal responsibility. When Obama entered the Oval Office in 2009, federal government debt stood at $10.6 trillion. By the time he left in 2017, it had nearly doubled to $19.9 trillion. Obama did so much damage that just two years into his term, Standard & Poor's lowered America's credit rating from AAA to AA+ ... for the first time since we first earned AAA status in 1917. In fact, the DINOs are so divorced from responsibility that The Learned Bartender of the Bronx, Alexandria Ocasio-Cortez, even said having the government *always* spend more than it has "absolutely" needs to be "a larger part of our conversation."

This is a recipe for disaster—and that's exactly what the Pigs here and abroad have in mind.

By spending money they don't have, spiking government debt to shocking levels, and stripping the dollar of value, DINOs are setting America up for a catastrophic fall. In fact, this fiscal crisis can only end one way if it isn't stopped: it will erode savings and investment, cause U.S. growth to stall, and heighten the economic (and national security) threat posed to America by our enemies.

Washington's federal debt is projected to reach nearly one and a half *times* the GDP by 2049, the year China aims to be the world's sole superpower. That's no coincidence. If DINOs keep gutting our currency, the Chinese yuan will replace the dollar as the world's benchmark. In fact, Saudi Arabia is already in talks with China about pricing its oil in yuan instead of dollars for the first time ever. Should this course continue and the yuan becomes the world's reserve currency, America won't be able to simply print more money to finance the federal government's debt, since other countries will no longer have any interest in or need for dollars. As a result, we'll be forced to sell our assets (land, companies, buildings, and more) to foreigners in order to finance the government's bloated budgets, and we'll be made to suffer the humiliation of austerity measures, just like other debt-ridden countries. Not coincidentally, we'll also be unable to protect allies like Taiwan from invasion by China because we'd effectively have to borrow money from China to wage war against it. And they won't be lending.

Already, America's families are struggling with higher prices, and American workers are seeing lower take-home income—but the "elites" are feeling no pain. That's because the rich rely on investments, not wages, for their income. And since inflation makes their investments more valuable (while pricing those same investments out of the reach of regular folks), the elites win. They know a sound dollar, fiscal responsibility, and the Trump era's low inflation are key to a strong American economy.

But because many of them work for and have a financial stake in China, its rise while America falls is just fine with them.

SORRY, WE'RE CLOSED.

"[We] have to stop ignoring this crisis in international trade. The longer we ignore it, the more American jobs will move overseas. It's just that simple."

Simple indeed. Those words, spoken by former Senator Byron Dorgan in 2004, didn't uncover a new Truth in economics. Instead, Dorgan articulated what everyone already knows: America's trade deals and government policies have been shipping American jobs to other countries like Mexico and China, leaving a decimated manufacturing base, vacant towns, and shattered lives in their wake.

No, what's notable about Senator Dorgan's warning isn't its policy but its politics. Byron Dorgan is a Democrat. Serving in the House and Senate for a total of thirty years, Dorgan was one of the last traditional Democrats in Congress before the DINOs completed their takeover of his party. That's why he's also remembered for saying, "This country needs to get a backbone and stand up for its economic interest."

Unfortunately, America's economic interest isn't what his party stands for now.

Consider our self-defeating trade deals. The North American Free Trade Agreement (NAFTA) is a heckuva place to start. Spearheaded by Bill Clinton, NAFTA eliminated tariffs existing between the U.S., Canada, and Mexico to create a massive trade zone. Clinton sold the deal by saying it would create a million new U.S. jobs over its first five years. But that was a lie. In fact, our trade deficit with Canada and Mexico grew *ten-fold*, costing us thousands of plants and upwards of a million jobs, especially in our once-robust automobile, auto parts, and electric appliance industries.

Not yet done, Clinton then inked legislation granting China permanent normal trade relations with us, despite their repeated acts of currency manipulation, corporate espionage, malicious hacking, and intellectual property theft. Once again, America's working families and industrial towns paid the price. Even the left-leaning Economic Policy Institute admitted this Clintonian blow cost millions of Americans their jobs.

Bethlehem Steel's massive furnace remains closed. Andrew Lichtenstein/ Corbis via Getty Images.

Today, many of our manufacturing centers lie barren. Industries that were created in America and once employed millions of our people have left our shores. For example, Americans invented semiconductors, a wide variety of appliances, and many types of consumer electronics, and we used to lead in their production. No longer. Our manufacturing strength has likewise been sapped in other key industries like steel, pharmaceuticals, heavy equipment, fertilizer, and apparel. America shouldn't be dependent on any other nation for anything. But today we are.

The grim truth is millions of our jobs were "offshored," meaning they were sent from America to other countries. They could have been kept in America for Americans, but the so-called elites decided otherwise. As a result, manufacturing accounts for less than 11% of America's economy today, down from more than 50% before the DINOs got started. Many millions of American jobs were destroyed by this carnage, according to the U.S. Bureau of Labor Statistics.

Meanwhile, manufacturing has surged in China and now accounts for approximately one-third of its economy. Adding insult to injury, all this occurred with the direct assistance of *our* government, which is supposed to be working for the U.S. taxpayers who fund it. For example, Senator Schumer stripped a Republican provision from the $280 billion CHIPS and Science Act passed in 2022, clearing the way for semiconductor research we fund here to be taken to China for chip production there.

That's why President Trump not only scrapped NAFTA for a better deal but also withdrew the U.S. from the Trans-Pacific Partnership (TPP). Pursued by Obama as one of his "legacy" achievements, TPP has been called "NAFTA on steroids" because it applied NAFTA's disastrous formula to America's trade with numerous Pacific Rim nations. Like NAFTA, it would have deepened America's trade deficit, which is directly linked to job loss here at home. Calling the destruction of U.S. jobs a "politician-made disaster," Trump rightly pinned it on "a leadership class that worships globalism over Americanism."

For the same reason, other DINO-backed efforts must be stopped. For example, Biden called for tariffs on Chinese imports to be dropped as a bizarre way to combat the inflation he created. Left unsaid, of course, is that doing so would flood the U.S. with even more Chinese products, causing additional American jobs to be lost. Similarly, tax hikes here push businesses (and their jobs) to other countries. As Chief Justice John Marshall wisely said more than 200 years ago, "The power to tax is the power to destroy." But though millions of American jobs have already been shipped elsewhere, the DINOs aren't done hurting us yet. In fact, there isn't a tax increase they wouldn't love to impose.

Washington's trade deals and tax hikes aren't the only threats facing us. The DINOs' response to COVID-19 is another textbook case of how Washington is destroying the American economy. In the pandemic's early days, many feared we were facing a modern-day equivalent of the Black Death, the plague that wiped out as many as 200 million people in the 14th century. Experts (ahem) breathlessly warned that many millions of Americans would be killed by COVID-19 and that people of all ages faced grave risk. As a result of these dire projections, equally dire restrictions were imposed. Lockdowns, curfews, and closure of businesses the elites deemed "nonessential" became the norm.

Pretty soon, though, it dawned on us the restrictions weren't just dire—they were demented. Major retailers like Amazon and Wal-Mart (who just so happened to have left-leaning lobbyists in Washington) were able to stay open, but hundreds of thousands of small businesses, which provide most of America's jobs, had to shut down. Did the COVID virus only exist in corner stores and family restaurants? Hardly.

Meanwhile, some of the people pushing these policies are doing very, very well. Take the vaunted Dr. Anthony Fauci, for instance, who mandated vaccines, boosters, and masks—only to contract COVID-19 himself (which sure makes you wonder). Believe it or not, Fauci is the single highest paid employee in the federal government, and he's not even a football coach! He raked in more than $434,000 in 2021—more than the President, Vice President, Generals, members of Congress, and every other federal employee. All told, his wealth is estimated at $10.4 million. And when he finally blesses us by retiring, he will continue to draw an annual pension of $414,667—the highest in government history.

With time, the world realized "experts" like Fat Cat Fauci had been wrong about a lot of things. Although the coronavirus released by the Wuhan Institute of Virology did indeed pose a very serious health risk, its feared death toll across all ages never materialized, thank God. Instead, we eventually learned the drastic measures imposed on us were without benefit. According to a bombshell report by The Johns Hopkins University: "We find no evidence that lockdowns, school closures, border closures, and limiting gatherings have had a noticeable effect on COVID-19 mortality." As delicately admitted by *The Lancet*, a highly respected peer-reviewed medical journal, experts' projections constituted "a significant overestimation."

But by that time, something else was realized—many small and mid-sized American businesses had been dealt a death blow by the government. An estimated one-third of all impacted businesses closed for good, impacting nearly half of America's private workforce, and many of those who somehow survived did so by scaling back their labor force. Meanwhile, the big-box stores kept growing, with a near monopoly in their markets and a thriving business delivering, you guessed it, Chinese-made products to Americans' homes.

That's not all. The DINOs in Washington came up with another whopper of an idea: pay people more money to remain idle than to get back to work. Specifically, they quadrupled the number of Americans deemed eligible for unemployment assistance, significantly lengthened the time such payments could be received, and added "bonuses" on top of unemployment benefits. The net result? An able-bodied man or woman could get $7.25 per hour (the federal minimum wage) by returning to work—or pocket the equivalent of $17.17 per hour by staying home. Americans are smart, so guess which door many of them chose....

Today, we have *millions* of open jobs in search of people to take them. In place of the productive engine that built America, the DINOs wedged in a bigger welfare state. Moreover, the labor shortage is causing wages to rise, and since wages have a big impact on the price of goods and services, this dynamic is fueling even more inflation. In a nutshell, all that made-up money the DINOs threw at the pandemic didn't revive the economy as they claimed it would—it stifled its recovery instead.

And now some DINOs from California want to make this pain permanent. Congressman Mark Takano and state Assembly members Evan Low and Cristina Garcia are trying to change the law so companies with 500 or more employees will have to shorten the workweek to four days—but still pay at the same rate they now do for five days of work. The Democrats who have authored this legislation call it "reimagining the workforce," but all it would really do is make American businesses even less of a threat to their competitors. Like those in China.

Taken together, these facts make something very clear: the DINOs are crippling our energy sector, driving us to recession, engaging in economic warfare, ratcheting up government debt, stripping the dollar of value, shipping jobs overseas, raising taxes, closing businesses, and expanding the welfare state. All of this is making America's economy weaker-but, rather than reverse course, the DINOs are doubling down.

Why? Check one:

☐ They are incompetent and don't mean to do this damage.

☐ It's merely a coincidence all this harm is happening now.

☐ They are working to weaken America-*according to plan*.

ATTACKING OUR MILITARY STRENGTH

"We maintain the peace through our strength;
weakness only invites aggression."

—PRESIDENT RONALD REAGAN

Peace through strength. For eons, that maxim has been proven true. Tribes, city states, nations, and alliances that were strong were less likely to be attacked. Those that were weak were vulnerable—and often vanquished.

So immutable is this reality that it was a central principle of President Reagan's military and foreign policy. During his two terms in office, the Soviet Union was armed to the teeth and aggressive against American interests. But Reagan didn't blanche—he built. And America's resulting strength protected our people and allies from harm without a single shot being fired.

Another unassailable truth is this: *those who appease ultimately get attacked.*

On March 12, 1938, Adolf Hitler annexed Austria—and the world didn't do a thing. Emboldened, he then bullied Western leaders six months later to get the Sudetenland, a key part of Czechoslovakia. He claimed this was "the last territorial demand I have to make in Europe." But of course, he was lying.

Adolf Hitler. Keystone-France/
Gamma-Keystone via Getty Images.

On March 15, 1939, Hitler sent his troops into the rest of Czechoslovakia and followed that aggression by invading Poland on September 1, 1939. In other words, just eighteen months after Hitler annexed Austria, he launched the invasion that plunged the world into war and resulted in the death of as many as 85,000,000 men, women, and children.

It's now clear all this would have been prevented had anyone stood up to this tyrant. Even then, some saw how costly appeasing Hitler would be. On October 5, 1938, Winston Churchill stood in Parliament's House of Commons and warned, "This is only the beginning of the reckoning. This is only the first sip, the first foretaste of a bitter cup which will be proffered to us year by year unless, by a supreme recovery of moral health and martial vigor, we arise again and take our stand for freedom as in the olden time."

But as the tragedy in Ukraine demonstrates, such a "stand for freedom" can be as unappealing to our leaders now as it was then.

Ukraine used to possess nuclear weapons and, thus, was a nation Russia dared not attack. This was crucially important to the Ukrainian people, whose national memory is scarred by the deaths of an estimated 10,000,000 Ukrainians from a famine engineered by Joseph Stalin. As a result, being a nuclear power meant being safe.

And then came Bill Clinton. In 1994, he brokered the Budapest Memorandum under which Ukraine would send its nukes to (wait for it) Russia. In return, the agreement assured the Ukrainian people that all nations would "respect the independence and sovereignty and the existing borders of Ukraine." Ha.

Peace prevailed under Clinton's successor, Republican President George W. Bush, but then came Barack Obama. In a manner eerily reminiscent of Hitler's move on Austria, Russia annexed Ukraine's rich Crimea region in 2014—with no response from Obama other than empty words and toothless sanctions.

Once again, alarm bells rang as critics declared America was emboldening Vladimir Putin by letting him loot Ukraine with impunity. But that's where historical events diverge. While Hitler was appeased by England's naïve Prime Minister, Neville Chamberlain, Obama can't be accused of naivete. Nor can his lack of action be attributed to stupidity, considering Obama's a smart guy with a Harvard law degree. Instead, this fits far too neatly with a "hot mic" incident I'll get to in a moment.

Put simply, Obama abandoned America's commitment to Ukraine and stood by while Putin's troops mobilized—because that's what Pigs do for each other. Let us never forget their quest is for power and profit, not peace.

After Donald Trump's unexpected win in 2016, Putin was compelled to bide his time (notwithstanding the fake news of

Trump-Russia collusion). But soon after Biden moved into the White House, Russia's assault began again. Russian troops amassed on Ukraine's border, causing Ukrainian President Volodymyr Zelenskyy to plead with Biden for help. None came, however, and Russian troop movements continued, culminating in Putin's full-scale invasion in February 2022.

As these photos of Mariupol, Ukraine show, the difference between strength and weakness is easy to see. One was taken during Trump's term and the other taken just fourteen months into Biden's.

Mariupol before Russian attacks. Elizaveta Becker\ ullstein bild via Getty Images.

Mariupol after Russian attacks. Maximilian Clarke/SOPA Images/ LightRocket via Getty Images.

As a result, one would expect (and fervently hope) our leaders are at least keeping America safe by keeping us strong. But as we'll soon see, it depends on who those leaders are and what their objectives appear to be. Spoiler alert: if they're hell-bent on weakening America so it can no longer be an obstacle to the Pigs, they'll do exactly what's being done to our nation right now.

WEAKENING OUR STATURE

*"From what happened in Afghanistan, [Taiwan] should
perceive that once a war breaks out in the Straits, the
island's defense will collapse in hours and the U.S.
military won't come to help."*

So wrote *The Global Times*, an official publication of the
Chinese Communist Party. The tabloid was speaking of Biden's
catastrophic withdrawal from Afghanistan, but its threat carries
far broader implications. "The US' epic defeat and chaotic retreat
in Afghanistan" offers an important lesson, CCP's newspaper
continued. "It cannot win a war anymore."

The U.S. cannot win a war anymore.

Consider a world in which those words are true. In such a
world, who will come to Taiwan's defense when China attacks?
Who will safeguard Israel from a second Holocaust? Who will
keep Russia from invading NATO countries? And who will
prevent North Korea from raining its missiles down on Seoul?
In other words, who will stop the Pigs from capturing and
controlling free people everywhere?

America's military has long earned its proud reputation.
Fighting for freedom, defending democracies, constructing
vital infrastructure, and returning home when the mission is
done. No other military of any other nation can lay claim to
the remarkable history and positive impact of our armed forces.
No one even comes close.

And that has made our military a prime target of those
seeking America's demise.

Biden's Afghanistan debacle is a painful case in point.
Promising a power transition that would be "responsible,

deliberate and safe," he instead fled the nation in an evacuation that was so chaotic, U.S. and Afghani servicemen lost their lives. The images of terrified Afghanis trying to flee with their American protectors brought back awful memories of Vietnam. Biden also left behind biometric data the Taliban is now using to find, torture, and kill Afghanis who helped us. He walked away from billions of dollars worth of taxpayer-funded facilities, including

A former U.S. helicopter displaying a Taliban flag. JAVED TANVEER/ AFP via Getty Images.

the U.S. embassy in Kabul and the modernized airbase at Bagram. And his abandonment of billions of dollars in advanced military equipment reverberated around the world, as fear of their use in terrorist attacks took hold.

Just as damaging as Biden's abandonment of Afghanistan was the loss of American leadership. The world watched in horror as Afghanis fell to their death from departing U.S. planes, but they were unable to watch the President—because he was AWOL. When Biden finally did reemerge, it wasn't to offer some clarity or to take accountability. Instead, he and his team made bizarre excuses for what happened.

But the message was clear: America was weak, unreliable, and leaderless.

Such injury to our stature has been repeated again and again by DINO administrations. When Bill Clinton was President, he sent U.S. forces to Somalia on what he called a humanitarian mission. Americans were then shocked by the sight of their finest being killed and mutilated by Somali gang members. Under

Barack Obama, America sent an apology and planeloads of cash to Iran after it took U.S. forces hostage. Obama's second term also saw China construct a chain of man-made islands in the South China Sea that packs such a military punch it "threatens all other nations in the region," according to Admiral Aquilino of the U.S. Indo-Pacific Command.

And Joe Biden? Although Afghanistan is bad enough, Biden's record of weakness extends well beyond it. He was irrelevant as Ukraine was invaded, with Putin evidently not caring at all about Biden's blather. He's demonstrated no resolve as China ramps up its naval maneuvers and hostile intrusions into Taiwan's airspace. He released from Guantanamo Bay the terrorist Mohammad al-Qahtani, who tried to enter America in order to participate in the 9/11 attacks. (Had Qahtani not failed to clear customs in Orlando, the plane he was ordered to help hijack would have had all five rather than four terrorists onboard—and would have crashed into the White House or Capitol instead of a Pennsylvania field.) And Biden shamefully terminated the China Initiative, which President Trump launched to counter Chinese espionage.

Little wonder, then, that Russia, China, Iran, and North Korea show little respect for Biden. And if our stature falls even further, one or more of them could become so emboldened as to put their disrespect into action, mounting multiple confrontations to the U.S. and the freedom she has historically defended.

Hours after the Taliban captured Kabul, CCP's *Global Times* provocatively asked, "If the U.S. cannot even secure a victory in a rivalry with small countries, how much better could it do in a major power game with China?" Given the harm now being inflicted on our standing in the world, it's a fair question.

WEAKENING OUR FORCES

"Develop the illusion that total disarmament [by] the
United States would be a demonstration of moral strength."
— *Communist Goal #3 (Congressional Record)*

I'm a big fan of moral strength, but if it's manipulated to serve as the false cover for unilateral disarmament, then the only possible outcome is America's cities will end up like Mariupol. To repeat, peace comes through strength, war is enabled by weakness. And that's why America's military is under constant attack by the DINOs.

Let's start with the government's investment in our nation's defense.

When Barack Obama declared an end to the Iraq War in 2011, U.S. defense spending totaled $855 billion. What followed can only be described as an assault on America's military. From 2011 through Obama's last year in office in 2016, defense spending fell to $682 billion, a decline so steep it slashed one out of every five dollars from our military. "Never before in history," Dinesh D'Souza observed, "has a global superpower disarmed itself so rapidly and so thoroughly."

Obama also purged the military of nearly 200 seasoned officers, not because they lacked the experience to protect our nation but because that's precisely what they wanted to do. "He's intentionally weakening and gutting our military," said former U.S. Army Major General Paul Vallely, "and anyone in the ranks who disagrees or speaks out is being purged."

Defense spending was at its lowest level in over a decade when Donald Trump entered the Oval Office in January 2017. By the time he left in 2021, nearly $2.9 trillion had been invested in our fighting forces. Thanks to his efforts, America was protected by the world's most powerful military, the Islamic caliphate had been destroyed, our NATO partners were ponying up more for the alliance's defense, and our friends were safe from aggression by Russia, China, North Korea, and Iran.

But it seems all this is deeply objectionable to DINOs.

Congressional Democrats (led by Rep. Barbara Lee of Communist Party fame) signed a letter in May 2020 urging cuts in President Trump's military spending. "In the last three years alone—during a time of relative peace—we have increased annual defense spending by more than $100 billion, almost 20 percent," they wrote. Knowing full well that peace is made possible by military strength, they wanted things to change. As a POLITICO headline put it, "Progressive lawmakers push to slash defense budget during pandemic." Dozens more joined Comrade Lee in making the same demand throughout 2021, signing onto letters that called for deep cuts in America's defense.

It seems they have a receptive ear in Joe Biden. Now that he's in the White House, the outlook for 2022 and 2023 is bleak. Naval experts are warning as many as 10,000 recruits may need to be canceled, and construction of essential naval vessels could be scrapped. America's Indo-Pacific Command requested $9.1 billion for 2023 to help it combat the rising Chinese threat, but Biden's Defense Department slashed that number by a third. As one news report put it, "The 2023 Defense Budget May Sink More Navy Ships Than Pearl Harbor." That's because Biden's 2023 budget calls for 24 ships to be decommissioned, 11 of which are not even 10 years old! Other than during Obama and Biden's presidencies, the Navy hasn't had a total active force level this low since 1916.

America risks falling behind on other crucial fronts too. Take hypersonic weapons, for example. These advanced missiles can deliver conventional and nuclear payloads at the speed of two miles per second. They're designed to blow past our defenses and can evade detection by traveling at lower trajectories. Here's the kicker: China, Russia, and even North Korea are now way ahead of the U.S. in this crucial technology. And if the DINOs continue to cut, we'll be rendered defenseless.

Meanwhile, China has *doubled* its military spending since 2011 and is "designing systems that are intended to defeat us," according to U.S. Air Force Secretary Frank Kendall.

The threat we face takes other forms, too. First, DINOs have dramatically reduced America's nuclear arsenal at the very same time other nations—most notably China, North Korea, and Iran—are building up theirs. Much of our disarmament came under Obama, who was caught on a "hot mic" telling then-Russian President Dmitriy Medvedev he'd be able to further cut America's missile defenses after the November 2012 elections. "This is my last election," he told Medvedev as they leaned in close to each other. "After my election, I have more flexibility." "I understand," Medvedev replied, with Obama patting his arm. "I transmit this information to Vladimir." Vladimir Putin, that is.

Second, rogue nations like North Korea and Iran are becoming an even more serious nuclear threat. In 2022, Kim Jong-un unveiled an intercontinental ballistic missile (ICBM) experts believe can reach the U.S. and nuke our cities. He has also announced that development of his nuclear arsenal is being accelerated, and North Korea's nuclear test site is being readied for use after being mothballed since 2018.

Meanwhile, Iran's nuclear program has been the beneficiary of Obama's Iran deal, which included sanctions relief worth up to $100 billion, some of which Iran has funneled to its anti-Israel terrorist proxies. In fact, the International Atomic Energy Agency confirms

"Iran has carried out activities relevant to the development of a nuclear device," such as increasing its uranium stockpiles, expanding its enrichment activities, and testing its missiles. Calling it "a horrible, one-sided deal that should have never, ever been made," Trump withdrew America from the Iran deal. No surprise, then, that the current DINO-in-Chief said he wants to reactivate the agreement, raising once more the frightening specter of a nuclear-armed Iran.

Iran's Supreme Leader Ayatollah Ali Khamenei. ATTA KENARE/ AFP via Getty Images.

And finally, our military is being hollowed out by "wokism." As Russian soldiers rape Ukraine and China tightens its grip around Taiwan, the Biden Administration is discharging thousands of our servicemen and women for the alleged offense of not being vaccinated. Just as extreme, service members have been deprived of a religious exemption from the vax mandate. And unvaccinated Air Force Academy cadets are being denied the commission as officers they worked so hard to achieve and may be required to pay back their tuition.

America's military is also being subjected to mandatory training on critical race theory, transgenderism, proper pronouns, political extremism, and climate change, among other non-military topics. So time-consuming is this diversion that the Senate Armed Services Committee estimates the Department of Defense has dedicated *millions* of hours to it just since Biden's term began. If you think this must surely relate to our military's mission of protecting the United States, just take a look at Defense Secretary Lloyd Austin's March 4, 2021 memo in which he ordered everyone in the Department of Defense to instead focus on tackling climate change, building safe spaces, and stamping out extremism in our military. In response, the Navy spent part of its budget producing a woke video featuring two sailors dressed in rainbows who gave instruction on how to use "proper gender pronouns" and "inclusive language." Not yet done, Biden's response to the *Dobbs* case reportedly includes expanding the mission of military bases—in pro-life states, they will now apparently also serve as abortion mills.

So, the Biden team is going woke as it cuts and disarms our forces, rejecting the time-honored truth of peace through strength and causing America and the free world to face ever more lethal threats. It appears Communist Goal #3 is well on its way to being achieved. Meanwhile, USO reports the suicide rate among active-duty members of the U.S. military is at an all-time high.

WEAKENING OUR BORDERS

"National security begins with border security.
Foreign terrorists will not be able to strike America
if they cannot get into our country."
—*President Donald Trump*

Immigration has been a thorny issue in America for years, particularly given the length of our borders. The U.S.-Mexico border spans nearly 2,000 miles, and the line separating America and Canada is the longest international border in the world, stretching more than 5,500 miles. Despite this enormous expanse, immigration into the United States has long been a largely legal affair.

When our nation was founded, immigrants were welcomed if they could support themselves. This common-sense framework meant people could come here to work and thrive, helping our nation build an economy of unprecedented size. And it became a core part of our national law when admission was formally barred to anyone who might become a "public charge" instead of a productive citizen. This approach honored the process of *legal* immigration, with decisions on who and how many to welcome based on the contribution they would make to America and her future. Coupled with a real commitment to the integrity of our borders, America's immigration policy resulted in three times as many people entering the U.S. legally than doing so illegally between 1990 and 2008.

Then Barack Obama entered the scene.

His administration decided it would not enforce our immigration laws. For example, Obama launched the Deferred Action for Childhood Arrivals (DACA) program, which permitted anyone up to a certain age who entered the U.S. illegally before their 16th birthday to stay. Called "DREAMers," they swelled to approximately 800,000 people and were allowed to access all sorts of taxpayer-funded benefits including health care, food supplies, drivers licenses, scholarships, and more.

U.S. President Barack Obama at DREAMer's press event. Olivier Douliery/ WHITE HOUSE POOL (ISP POOL IMAGES)/ Corbis/VCG via Getty Images.

Obama claimed their stay would be temporary but, once it was underway, he changed his tune. "These kids are Americans just like us," he said in 2015, "and they belong here." His fellow DINOs clearly agreed because after President Trump rescinded the program, they pushed to enable DREAMers to become U.S. citizens. All told, an estimated 2,500,000 people entered the U.S. illegally during Obama's time in the White House.

That's why Donald Trump made border security a key part of his campaign. We're all familiar with the border wall he built, but that's just the most visible aspect of his immigration agenda. Trump also beefed up border personnel and implemented the "Remain in Mexico" policy, which required migrants to wait in Mexico while their asylum application is processed. He also restricted travel from high-risk countries, increased worksite enforcement, cracked down on "birth tourism," and sent a clear message to all would-be lawbreakers: if you want to come to America, obey the law and do it the way millions of legal immigrants have done it before you. As a direct result, encounters with those seeking illegal entry dropped by 64% overall during his time in office and by an astounding 80% among those coming from El Salvador, Guatemala, and Honduras.

And then came Joe Biden.

In short order, he reversed course to an extent not even his staunchest critics could have predicted. On his very first day in office, he signed orders suspending deportations of illegal aliens. He put an end to "Remain in Mexico," halted construction of the border wall, and paid billions to contractors *not* to continue building it. He loudly condemned mounted border guards for whipping migrants and then went silent when it was confirmed they weren't. He also scrapped the announced illegals would receive official ID cards, and ordered Border Patrol officers to help illegals enter the U.S. instead of removing them. The situation has become so bad an agent told Project Veritas, "There's no one patrolling the border."

Perhaps most alarming, however, are Biden's "ghost flights." So named because they occur at night when few people are in airports to serve as witnesses, these flights take illegal immigrants from the southern border to towns and cities all around America. According to information the Department of Homeland Security was compelled to provide to Congress, tens of thousands of illegals have already been transported on these ghost flights for resettlement in communities across America. None of this is free, of course, and U.S. taxpayers have reportedly been hit with costs exceeding $1.5 billion.

Not surprisingly, Biden's open border policies have led to an explosion in the number of people entering America illegally. As of this writing, an estimated 2,000,000 illegals (some wearing Biden t-shirts) crossed the border seeking asylum during his first year in office, and another 2,500,000 are projected for 2022. If this keeps up, the total number is expected to exceed 11,350,000 during Biden's 4-year term. And since the Border Patrol estimates two illegals (known as *gotaways*) enter and run for every one who seeks asylum, the total number of "Bidenistas" illegally entering America thanks to his open borders could exceed 30,000,000! All told, Texas Lieutenant Governor Dan Patrick estimates one out of every five people in the U.S. will be illegal after just four years of the Biden presidency. Think about that.

Taken together, this means Joe Biden has turned Barbara Jordan's words upside down. You'll recall she said, "For our immigration policy to make sense, it is necessary to make distinctions between those who obey the law, and those who violate it." Under Biden, distinctions are certainly being made all right: those who obey the law get screwed while those who violate it get served. American citizens abroad were told they must have a negative COVID-19 test or proof of recovery before they could fly back to their home in the States—illegals can stroll right in. Americans were told to socially distance—illegals caravan in large groups. Americans who aren't vaccinated have lost their jobs and livelihoods—illegals who aren't vaccinated are welcomed and flown all over America. DINO-led cities imposed indoor mask mandates—COVID-infected illegals are promised entry without any Title 42 impediment.

But illegals and infections aren't alone in crossing the border. Violent crime and lethal drugs are coming here, too, along with human traffickers, known terrorists, and drug dealers.

Human trafficking has become big business as cartels get paid for transporting migrants and children into America. The reports of their mistreatment, including frequent sexual assault, are heartbreaking. Meanwhile, thousands of Americans have been raped, robbed, and killed by criminals who enter our nation illegally. Reports also indicate Hezbollah cells are now in place throughout Latin America, enabling Iran to bring war to our doorstep. Terrorists are also entering the U.S., including some classified as a "Tier 1" threat and officially listed as "Armed and Dangerous." In fact, more than 50 of them are on the FBI's terror watch list. (To put that number into perspective, the 9/11 attack was committed by 19 terrorists.)

On top of all that, Biden's open border is allowing in a flood of fentanyl, a murderous synthetic heroin that is being shipped here by China via Mexican cartels. How big is the Biden Body Count so far? Experts estimate more than 100,000 Americans died from fentanyl between April 2020 and April 2021 alone. Pause for a moment to let the significance of 100,000 sink in.

It means more Americans have lost their lives to this Chinese drug in a single year than died in the forty-two years of the Vietnam, Iraq, and Afghanistan Wars. Combined. And fentanyl is estimated to be killing another 300 daily, which is equivalent to losing one jumbo jet full of Americans every single day.

As a result, fentanyl is now the *leading* cause of death among 18-to-45-year-old Americans. Just as shocking, the amount of fentanyl law enforcement has seized could kill every man, woman, and child in America. And yet, even more of it is getting through our open border and poisoning our people on a daily basis.

Given the staggering death count, violent crime, and rates of infection that are resulting from Biden's open border, surely he and the DINOs would be rushing to reverse course, right? No, and don't hold your breath either because the Pigs have a plan here, too.

You see, open borders are a key part of their quest for globalism. Mass migration is only possible with open borders, and open borders are essential to the formation of a global "community" controlled by an all-powerful ruling class. That's why DINOs are dismantling any semblance of America's border. It's also why so much money is being invested in their efforts by George Soros and his aptly-named Open Society Foundations, which boasts the second-largest financial war chest of any private foundation in America.

In addition, the DINOs are counting on every illegal who's come here courtesy of Obama and Biden to vote for them. That's why *every single* Democrat in the Arizona Senate opposed legislation requiring proof of citizenship before a person can vote. It's why Democrats in leftist-run states like California, Massachusetts, New York, and Washington have become "sanctuaries" for illegals. It's why California became the first state in America to guarantee free health care for illegals. And it's why Nancy Pelosi's cynically-named "For The People Act" would require states to automatically add to the voting rolls anyone—including illegals—who gets government benefits. Neat trick, that.

For the Pigs, violating Barbara Jordan's vision isn't just desirable. It's essential. Because despite how weak the open border makes America or how many lives it's already shattered, the DINOs are driven by their singular purpose: power.

Looking back at this chapter, it's undeniable: our military is being weakened by spending cuts, unilateral disarmament, and "woke" politics. We are surrendering to thugs, being disrespected by our enemies, letting in terrorists, and losing American lives to the brutality of open borders. All of this is making America's defenses weaker-but, rather than reverse course, once again the DINOs are doubling down.

Why? Check one:

☐ They are incompetent and don't mean to do this damage.

☐ It's merely a coincidence all this harm is happening now.

☐ They are working to weaken America-*according to plan.*

ATTACKING OUR SOCIAL STRENGTH

"A house divided against itself cannot stand."

Drawing from Mark 3:25, Abraham Lincoln expressed this truth at the Illinois Republican State Convention in 1858. Why there? Well, as left-leaning teachers curiously neglect to tell their students, Lincoln was among the Republican Party's first members. Created in 1854, the party's founding platform must have strongly appealed to him, since six of its nine planks called for slavery to be abolished and African Americans' equal rights to be protected. For that reason too, Lincoln was one of the Republican Party's first candidates for the Presidency.

As Lincoln warned against "a house divided," America faced a perilous choice: would she rid the evil institution of slavery from every inch of her land, or would it spread like a disease and consume the entire nation? As far as Lincoln was concerned, keeping it in some states but not in others wasn't on the table.

Something so hideous either had to be destroyed…or it would become America's destroyer.

More than a century and a half later, America once again confronts perilous choices. Slavery stands apart as a uniquely horrifying institution, but other threats are now pulling at our society's seams. Will our people be united or divided? Will our children be educated or indoctrinated? Will our families thrive or fall apart? And will our communities be safe or assaulted by crime?

Each of these questions is monumentally important because the wrong answer could demolish much of what makes America special and free.

To build and sustain her strong communities, America relies on family, education, and the fundamentals of a civil society. But those bonds are now being perilously weakened. Seeking America's demise, our enemies actively foment social division, educational failure, family breakdown, and violent crime. The result is a nation being split apart as children grow up with hatred or guilt in their hearts, receive poor and perverted education, live without one or both parents, and are unsafe on their own streets.

Part IV will focus on how we can come together and save our great nation. But first, we need to take an unflinching look at what the Left is doing to tear her apart.

DIVISION AND DUNCE CAPS

"Not 'God Bless America.' God Damn America!"

That's toxic stuff, and it wasn't spewed by just anyone. Rev. Jeremiah Wright preached those words to Barack Obama and other parishioners from his pulpit at Chicago's Trinity United Church of Christ. If Rev. Wright's name sounds familiar, it's because he also officiated the Obamas' wedding and baptized their two daughters.

As a result, his hate-filled and hateful words deserve our attention.

A sentiment like Wright's can't help but split people apart. And that's the point. After all, if we're set upon one another, we can't be unified. If we're taught to hate our country, we won't defend her. And if we end up a divided, mis-educated mess, we'll be easy pickings for those who want to create crisis and assert control.

This is exactly what our enemies have been working to accomplish. They're separating us by fomenting racial tension, and they're suppressing us by propagandizing our children. Let's examine both.

FROM UNITY, DIVISION

Recall what JFK said about racial policy: "We are too mixed, this society of ours, to begin to divide ourselves on the basis of race or color." Are things so very different, sixty years after he made this point? The Left wants you to think so. America, they never tire of telling us, is systemically racist.

But from the nation's Capitol to many of its smallest towns, blacks hold positions of influence and authority. This is the nation that elected an African American as President. Twice. And it's where blacks and Hispanics have served as Cabinet members, Attorneys General, and Supreme Court Justices. In fact, members of America's ethnic and racial minorities fill a vast array of public positions, including lawmakers, chiefs of police, and judges. They are also entrepreneurs and business owners, scientists and millionaires, celebrities and medical professionals.

Here's what DINOs don't want you to know: racial, ethnic, and religious differences that often lead to bloodshed elsewhere aren't given a second thought here. Protestants and Catholics, Muslims and Jews, rich and poor and, yes, blacks and whites all work, live, and shop here—side by side. So do those from nations like India and Pakistan, who are enemies there but neighbors here. That's why Dennis Prager was absolutely right when we wrote, "We are the most successful experiment in creating a multiracial, multi-ethnic, multi-religious country in world history." The fact is, a rich diversity of people come together in America to pursue their dreams, serve in our armed forces, marry and raise children, and cheer on their hometown teams. And as they do so, they embody the mixed society President Kennedy was talking about.

Here's something else DINOs want to keep hidden: their party's own sordid history with racism. Democrats were the party of slavery, which is why abolitionists formed the Republican Party with a strong anti-slavery platform and elected Abraham Lincoln as America's first Republican president. Democrats are also the reason President Trump proposed the Juneteenth holiday, honoring June 19, 1865, when Union troops arrived in Texas and enforced the Emancipation Proclamation, which had been issued by Lincoln two and a half years earlier but kept under wraps by Texas Democrats. Even now, DINOs talk anti-racism but fail to practice it. For example, Republican Congressman Louie Gohmert twice offered a privileged resolution on the floor of the House of Representatives that would ban from Congress any political party that ever publicly supported slavery. The Democratic Majority, led by Speaker Pelosi, quashed his resolution—because it would have applied to them.

Most of all, DINOs absolutely, positively don't want you to know that racism and diversity aren't at the top of minorities' list of priorities—not by a long shot. A diverse group of community leaders came together to form Color Us United, a wonderful organization advocating against those seeking to divide Americans by race. Also of particular note, an April 2022 survey by Pew Research asked black American adults for the ten issues that most concern them and their community. Violence/Crime and Economic Issues topped the list at numbers one and two. Where was Racism/Diversity/Culture? Near the bottom in the ninth slot, ranking even behind "No issues" which came in seventh!

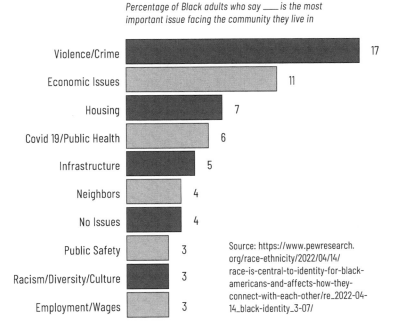

Percentage of Black adults who say ___ is the most important issue facing the community they live in

Issue	Percentage
Violence/Crime	17
Economic Issues	11
Housing	7
Covid 19/Public Health	6
Infrastructure	5
Neighbors	4
No Issues	4
Public Safety	3
Racism/Diversity/Culture	3
Employment/Wages	3

Source: https://www.pewresearch.org/race-ethnicity/2022/04/14/race-is-central-to-identity-for-black-americans-and-affects-how-they-connect-with-each-other/re_2022-04-14_black-identity_3-07/

We have further to travel, to be sure, but it cannot be denied we've come a very, very long way. And yet, denying our progress is exactly what the Left is determined to do.

They are working hard to divide us in the name of diversity. They charge the U.S. is not only racist, it's *systemically* so. Every challenge isn't something to be overcome, it's something to blame on racism. And no student should emerge from our schools without a head full of this nonsense. Left unsaid, though, is any answer to this question: if America is so racist, why are so many people of color clamoring to come in—and so few trying to get out?

In the name of identity politics and multiculturalism, the Left has concocted a narrative that says Americans of all races are so different and so at odds with each other, we simply cannot find common ground. You see, Leftists know racial harmony is their enemy because a united people is unwilling to be fleeced and unable to be conquered. So, they keep sewing division instead of unity. As the internationally acclaimed economist, Thomas Sowell, pointed out, "Racism is not dead, but it is on life support—kept alive by politicians, race hustlers and people who get a sense of superiority by denouncing others as 'racists'."

In the heart of the nation's Capital city, Georgetown University Provost Robert Groves puts it this way: "Diversity is the one thing we all have in common." That's right, the *one* thing. Groves is apparently unaware that our creed—*E Pluribus Unum*—literally means "Out of Many, One." We Americans, he and his ilk contend, don't even have our nationality in common. Nope, the only thing we share is that we're different from each other.

This claptrap can be found just about everywhere these days, but perhaps nowhere is it so forcefully advanced as in America's classrooms.

SCHOOLS FOR A WEAKER SOCIETY

Every fall, school doors open, and a new batch of bright, eager kindergartners runs in. All of them hold promise. All can grow up to be anything they set their hearts and minds to become.

But within ten years, millions of those smart, happy kids will be beaten down, their hopes forgotten, their expectations diminished, and their anger ready to blow at a moment's notice.

What happened to those kindergartners? Failing schools happened.

America's education system was intended to be exceptional. The Department of Education's mission captures this objective well: "To promote student achievement and preparation for global competitiveness by fostering educational excellence and ensuring equal access." That's why America's schools are free and open to all.

But meeting this mission has become a different story. Sixty years ago, American students consistently ranked at the top of international comparisons in math, reading, and science. Since then, schools have dropped so far and become so woke, it's fair to ask whether they are ripping us off. Since the National Elementary and Secondary Education Act was passed as part of the Great Society in 1965, America has spent more than *$4 trillion* on K-12 education. That's more money than any other nation has spent on education. In fact, no other country comes close. In 2022 alone, more than $700 billion was spent on public schools. And yet, they keep failing the children they are supposed to teach.

The problem, you see, isn't the amount of money we're spending—it's what we're spending it on. Instead of the productive and patriotic education American schools used to provide, our kids are now being subjected to political indoctrination.

In Seattle, for example, the K-12 teaching guidelines insist math is racist. The wokesters there contend "math has been and continues to be used to oppress and marginalize people and communities of color." You read that right. Or consider

Washington, DC, where the public school system receives more than $20,000. Per student. And yet, more than 1-in-3 DC public high school students either don't graduate on time or drop out altogether, and more than 9-in-10 of those who remain haven't learned enough to score as proficient in math. Nationwide, the Department of Education estimates more than 40 million American adults are so poorly schooled they would have trouble reading this page—or wouldn't be able to do it at all. Which means the alleged educators now staffing the Department are utterly failing to meet its mission.

As former Secretary of State Colin Powell rightly declared, this is "more than a problem. It is a catastrophe."

Which brings us to Critical Race Theory (CRT), a construct sprung directly from Marxism. Consistent with their quest to drive Americans apart, DINOs and their comrades in the education establishment are filling students' heads with some pretty awful stuff. America, our kids are "taught," is systematically oppressive and racist. According to the infamous 1619 Project, America was founded not to conceive a nation in liberty but to sustain slavery. Somehow, the lecturers neglect to mention that America didn't even exist in 1619, so the slavery that took place here was conducted by European powers. They also skip right past the fact that America's founding in 1776 made it possible for slavery to be abolished here, which more than half of our new nation's states soon did. Instead, the CRT cretins pound into students that the only way to correct for America's apparent sins is to see all Americans as either oppressors or the oppressed, discriminate against white males, and change the 3 Rs from reading, writing, and arithmetic to regrets, recrimination, and reparations.

And then there's Comprehensive Sexuality Education (CSE). Concocted by the globalists at the United Nations Educational,

Scientific and Cultural Organization (UNESCO), CSE brings graphic sexual materials into classrooms of kids as young as five—all without parents being informed. The depraved nature of CSE is evident in just a few of its many examples. *Six* year olds in New York City first grade classrooms have been taught how to masturbate. *Ten* year olds in Chicago schools are given condoms. Transvestites come into libraries for "drag queen story hours" where they read their material to young children. And "transition closets" have been set up in elementary, middle, and high schools, where students can change into alternative clothing without their parents' knowledge.

Before their party was hijacked by the Far Left, Democrats would have been horrified by the notion of CSE, but DINO leaders are all over it. For example, Michigan Attorney General Dana Nessel is calling for there to be "a drag queen for every school." Not to be outdone, Nancy Pelosi appeared on RuPaul's *Drag Race All Stars* show to claim drag "is what America is all about." And President Biden issued an executive order directing the Department of Health and Human Services to ramp up the delivery of "gender-affirming" healthcare services—to children.

The sexualization and grooming of our kids is as dangerous as it is disturbing. It has included a "drag your kids to pride" drag show in Dallas during which children gave dollar bills to drag queens as a neon sign displayed the message, "IT'S NOT GONNA LICK ITSELF!" And it has led to acts of sexual violence like the rape of a 14-year-old Virginia student by a boy wearing a skirt who had free entry into the girls' school bathroom. But leftists are so wed to this depraved ideology that former White House Press Secretary Jen Psaki called "horrific" a Florida law protecting five-, six-, and seven-year-olds from explicit sexual content!

When teacher unions demanded that schools be shut down for COVID, students brought their school books home. Parents were shocked to discover they were filled with CRT and CSE. Thousands of teachers across the country are using this garbage instead of actually fulfilling the Department of Education's mission. And the Department itself diverted billions in COVID relief funds to CRT training for teachers (and then lied about it). The results—traumatized children and race-based division—are the evidence we're being ripped off.

But once again, none of this should come as a surprise. Lenin revealed the plan when he said, "Give me four years to teach the children and the seed I have sown will never be uprooted." Hitler agreed: "Let me control the textbooks and I will control the state." So did the Communist Party Education Workers [aka: teachers] Congress. "We must create out of the younger generation a generation of Communists," they declared. "We must remove the children from the crude influence of their families. We must take them over and, to speak frankly, nationalize them."

These evil efforts spell doom for America if they are allowed to continue. Thomas Sowell, for example, was raised in Harlem where he received an excellent education because the Left had not yet taken over its schools. Reflecting on the damage done since then, he said "Ours may become the first civilization destroyed, not by the power of our enemies, but by the ignorance of our teachers and the dangerous nonsense they are teaching our children. In an age of artificial intelligence, they are creating artificial stupidity."

And that's precisely what we face today. We now have a generation of young Americans whose training in Science, Technology, Engineering, and Mathematics (STEM) can't hold a candle to China's…but who can recite chapter and verse about the evils of America. We also have an education establishment that's not only abusing our children but is violating Rev. Martin Luther King Jr.'s vision of equal education. How? By preventing poor and minority parents from doing what the elites (including the Clintons, Obamas, Bidens, and Pelosis) do all the time: escape failing public schools and send their kids to better private ones instead.

In the landmark *Brown v. Board of Education* decision prohibiting school segregation, Chief Justice Earl Warren wrote, "It is doubtful that any child may reasonably be expected to succeed in life if he is denied the opportunity of an education." No one knows this better than the Left. And our kids' and nation's low prospects for success are exactly what they have in mind.

FIGHTING THE FAMILY

"We disrupt the Western-prescribed nuclear family."
*"We support reforms that restructure
gender and cultural relationships."*

Search the Black Lives Matter website, and you won't find the first of these damning statements. The reason, though, isn't that BLM is pro-family. No, it's because they're anti-bad press. Long featured on the "What We Believe" page of BLM's website, these words were then scrubbed in 2020 as the group saw criticism rise and its poll numbers drop. But their inclusion in the first place is meaningful because BLM co-founders Patrisse Cullors and Alicia Garza are self-described "trained Marxists." As a result, they were likely taught Karl Marx's *Communist Manifesto*, in which he wrote about "Abolition of the family!"

A search for the second statement will be more successful. As of this writing, it continues to be prominently displayed by the Democratic Socialists of America on their website (yes, the very same DSA to which many of the Far-Left DINOs in Congress belong). In similar fashion, one of the 45 Communist Goals for America plainly states:

> #40. Discredit the family as an institution. Encourage promiscuity and easy divorce.

But why should the Far Left be so anti-family? Families, after all, are the foundation of healthy societies. When the majority of a community's members belong to family units, they are more stable, productive, prosperous, and involved in the lives of their children.

Ahh, that's why: families play the role Leftists envision for the State.

You see, Hilary Clinton and her cronies honestly believe "it takes a village to raise a child." Not a stable, two-parent family—a "village." Which is to say, the collective. If families are strong, the need for government is weak. But if families can be made weak, the result is people in need. And that's a need tailor-made for socialists and their dream of all-powerful government.

HOW FAR WE'VE FALLEN

When America's post-WWII Baby Boom reached its zenith in 1960, the two-parent nuclear family that BLM and DSA hate was our nation's most common family type. Nearly three-quarters of all kids lived in homes with two parents who weren't just married—they were in their first marriage. Today, fewer than half of American children do. Overall, nearly 90% of all American kids lived in families headed by two parents. That number has since fallen to less than 70%. Back in the day, more than 4-in-10 American households were nuclear families. Today's number is nearly 50% lower.

The statistics are equally grim when it comes to divorce. In 1960, just 9.2 of 1,000 marriages ended in divorce. Since then, the divorce rate has more than doubled. Even worse, more than 40% of the marriages taking place in 2022 are projected to end in divorce. At the same time, the sanctity of marriage is taking a beating, as the number of American parents who are unmarried has soared from just 1-in-20 in 1960 to 1-in-4 today.

Today's fragmented families also bear a heavy economic strain. Two parent families enjoy higher earnings than men and women without a partner. In fact, poverty strikes just 7.5% of married couples with children. By contrast, single parent families are much more likely to be poor, with 25% of families headed by single men and nearly 40% of families headed by single women falling into poverty.

Crime is another consequence of the breakdown of the American family. Hillary got it all wrong: absent the nurturing love of a mom and dad, kids suffer tremendously. America has more fatherless kids than any other nation in the world, and as the number of fatherless families has risen, so too has violent crime. Numerous analyses have been done on this subject, and their findings are unsurprisingly consistent. Simply put, many of the kids raised in broken homes commit criminal acts. A Heritage Foundation study, for example, discovered juvenile crime rises by 17% for every 10-point increase in kids living with just one parent. The importance of family is underscored by another finding: even in the most crime-ridden communities, fewer than 10% of kids raised by both parents commit a crime—but just 10% of those from unstable homes avoid doing so.

"FOR THE CHILDREN"

All this leaves America's kids and future at great risk. And that's just the way the Left wants it. You see, even though Nancy Pelosi cloyingly claims to be "for the children," she and her fellow DINOs have aggressively pursued policy changes that directly undermine families.

Consider the "Great Society." Launched by President Lyndon Johnson in the 1960s, it spawned nearly one hundred government programs that, all told, have consumed more than $23 trillion. This staggering amount equals fully two-thirds of federal government debt, and much of that spending was destructive. For example, Johnson's War on Poverty generated larger welfare checks to recipients who had children but weren't married, creating perverse incentives that replaced intact families with a skyrocketing number of out-of-wedlock births. No longer were fathers fiscally responsible for their children—the government would pick up the tab. Combined with no-fault divorce (gutting "until death do us part" vows) and on-demand abortion (devaluing the miracle of human life), such social engineering took a direct hit on American families.

But that wasn't enough for the DINOs. It's well known that stable incomes promote stable households and that many of those suffering job loss end up splitting apart. But rather than promote employment, DINOs push for trade deals and regulatory burdens that send American jobs overseas, leaving in their wake shuttered factories and broken homes. Likewise, instead of reducing taxes to enable every family dollar to stretch further (as JFK favored), they ratchet up every conceivable levy until even working families can't make ends meet. Last but by no means least, they promote radical "education" that lampoons the traditional family while lauding just about everything else.

The result is spelled out in statistics and sadness. After decades of assault, millions of America's families are falling apart. But don't expect the Left to alter course. Far from it. In response to the pain their cruel agenda itself has caused, DINOs push for more and more welfare spending—the government gleefully stepping in where independent, self-sufficient, two-parent families thrived not so long ago.

Morgan Zegers, CEO of Young Americans Against Socialism, put it this way: "The left's attack on the nuclear family, all goes into that growing support for socialism, that collectivist mindset that we're seeing in America." She's right, and that's precisely their plan.

FROM CRIME, CHAOS

"The fight to defund policing continues."
—*Rep. Alexandria Ocasio-Cortez (D-NY)*

As Antifa and BLM riots plunged U.S. cities into chaos in 2020, the nation's homicide rate rose by the largest year-over-year increase in more than 100 years.

And then came 2021.

In that year, more than 550 people were murdered—in Philadelphia alone. On average, more than 10 Philadelphians were killed each week, resulting in the highest body count ever before seen in "the city of brotherly love." But Philadelphia was by no means alone. Urban areas across America suffered historic losses to murder in 2021.

This misery extends to other crimes too. That same year, the number of rapes reached 28,000, aggravated assaults numbered 921,612, and armed robberies surged to 41,937. Looting took off too, as street riots and so-called "autonomous zones" opened the door wide for lawlessness.

But it wasn't always this way. In the decades leading up to the 1960s, the nation's murder rate actually *fell* dramatically. By 1960, it was less than half what it had been in the mid-1930s. Black homicide rates alone fell by more than 20% in the 1950s. Not coincidentally, the poverty rate among blacks also fell by nearly 50% between 1940 and 1960, as America's rising tide and stable families lifted boats of every color.

But then the Left got going. Jobs and communities were decimated, and the murder rate sharply reversed course, rising by more than 75% in a decade and doubling by the end of the 1970s. Fueling this rise were new policies curtailing law enforcement and allowing violent criminals back on the street. Other key contributors were the breakdown of the family and teen enlistment in street gangs for a sense of belonging and security. Add to those factors the violence that erupted as the drug trade took off, and the inevitable result was an explosion in crime and a heartbreaking number of victims.

If these failures sound uncomfortably familiar, they should—the same policies pushed by the Far Left fifty years ago have returned with a vengeance.

Leftists know that enforcement of laws leads to compliance with them. And compliance with laws leads to peace and prosperity. But peaceful and prosperous communities aren't susceptible to socialism. As Mao said, "When the worst chaos emerges, that is when the greatest control can be achieved." So, the Left seeks chaos, not calm—meaning law enforcement has to go.

As a result, Antifa and BLM are waging a war on law enforcement with a little help from their Far-Left friends in politics and media, as well as deep-pocketed backers like George Soros. The police must be defunded, we were told. They are racists, homophobes, and misogynists. They must be retrained, restrained, and reimagined (whatever that means). They should lose qualified immunity protection and be exposed to lawsuits by any criminal who objects to having been arrested.

Never mind that a total of more than 22,000 law enforcement officers have heroically given their lives in the line of duty. Or that the number of police officers murdered rose nearly 60% in 2021. Or even that, on average, more than 150 policemen and women are assaulted every day. Forget all that. Their budgets must be slashed, their integrity maligned, and their very purpose—keeping the peace—condemned.

Unsurprisingly, DINO-led "blue" cities and states joined the fray, cutting police budgets, doing little to protect officers from harm, and driving many of them away. In Los Angeles alone, the 2020 police department budget was slashed by $150 million, causing its staffing to fall to a level not seen in more than a decade. New York City Mayor Bill DeBlasio went even further. Flush with Soros' endorsement and financial support, he slashed $1 billion from the New York Police Department's budget for 2021.

Other "reimagined" policies were foisted on the public, too. The DINO-dominated California legislature, for example, passed Proposition 47, the perversely named "Safe Neighborhoods and Schools Act." Among its many toxic provisions is this: anyone who wants to steal someone else's property doesn't have to worry about being prosecuted for anything other than a petty misdemeanor—just make sure the stuff you steal isn't worth more than $950. Seriously.

Just as hazardous, "woke" prosecutors (many elected with campaign cash donated by George Soros) refuse to prosecute and jail criminals. These efforts are multiplied by the millions Soros has funneled through the "Poor People's Campaign," a radical initiative that marched on Washington in June 2022. Seeking to eliminate criminal penalties for violent protestors and rioters, these prosecutors contribute to lawlessness by treating lawbreakers as if they were the victims. They release violent criminals, many of whom strike again, and add yet another reason for police officers to simply give up.

As David Horowitz, a former progressive himself, recently wrote, Republicans get it all wrong when they describe Democrats as 'soft on crime':

> Democrats are not soft on crime. They are pro-crime: Democrat prosecutors have systematically refused to prosecute violent criminals; Democrat mayors and governors have released tens of thousands of violent criminals from America's prisons, and abolished cash bail so that criminals are back on the streets immediately after their crimes and arrests; Democrat mayors supported the mass violence orchestrated by Black Lives Matter in 220 cities in the summer of 2020, provided bail for arrested felons, de-funded police forces, and instructed law enforcement to stand down in Democrat-run cities, which allowed "protesters" to loot and burn, and criminal mobs to loot and destroy downtown shopping centers.

Horowitz is right. We used to keep our communities safe by throwing the book at criminals—now, woke prosecutors are making everyone more vulnerable by tossing a pillow at them. Sadly, the result of all this is as predictable as it was planned.

Underpaid and unappreciated, many officers have given up. For example, the Law Enforcement Legal Defense Fund reports 1-in-10 officers departed the force in Cleveland, Ohio, 1-in-11 did so in Austin, Texas, and 1-in-12 left Las Vegas. Seattle found itself with so few detectives, in fact, it was unable to investigate rapes and other adult sexual assaults. And with fewer police on the beat, crime exploded.

New York City saw more homicides after DeBlasio's 2020 cuts than in the prior two years—combined. Retailers in California and elsewhere began being regularly hit by "smash and grab" looters. These flash mobs descend on stores, destroy property, steal everything they can grab, and terrorize staff and shoppers. Their loot then shows up on sidewalk stands down the street, where the thieves brazenly sell their stolen merchandise, confident their state's $950 rule and decimated police force insulate them from prosecution for their crimes.

In similar fashion, Antifa thugs took to the streets. Cowardly covered in black clothes and masks, they smashed and looted stores, beat up innocent bystanders, and set fire to scores of police cars and city buildings. According to the Center for Strategic and International Studies, Antifa members are "far-left militants" who "blend anarchist and communist views." Delightful.

And then there are the BLM riots. Americans were urged by reporters to ignore the fires raging behind them—what we were seeing on TV were in fact "peaceful protests." Right. In reality, businesses and city blocks were torched, devastating minority and low-income communities. Murders, rapes, and looting were committed. Police vehicles were torched by rioters, including two who used a Molotov cocktail and yet have curiously been given lenient sentences. And BLM organizers were there every step of the way (when they weren't hanging out in their $6 million LA mansion, that is), participating in 95% of the hundreds of incidents defined as riots by Princeton's Crisis Monitor.

Burned building during a protest in Minneapolis, May 30, 2020. Shay Horse/NurPhoto via Getty Images.

Also rushing in are those promoting illegal drug use. As previously discussed, China and the Mexican cartels are flooding America with fentanyl, causing hundreds of thousands of deaths here. On top of that, some of those engaged in fentanyl trafficking are being treated as if they were transporting Fanta instead. A California court, for example, released two men in June 2022 just a day after they were caught with more than 150,000 fentanyl pills.

At the same time, DINOs are working hard to legalize marijuana, a hazardous drug that harms brain development (making America less competitive) and that has been confirmed by the CDC to be a gateway to other dangerous substances. And the Biden Administration announced it would spend millions providing "safe smoking kits" so people could (wait for it) *safely* break the law by smoking an illegal drug, crack cocaine.

This is destructive. But once again, don't lose any sleep on behalf of the Pigs. They're doing just fine. The ruling class has extensive security to protect them, much of it at taxpayer expense of course. And when that's not enough to make them feel safe, they can simply erect special barriers and call up the National Guard, as Nancy Pelosi shamelessly did when she felt threatened by, umm, the American people. The tree-lined streets where their large homes are located are an oasis from crime too, thanks to police, walls, security cameras, and more.

Meanwhile, the city in which many of them "work" is teetering on the verge of collapse. In 2021 alone, 226 residents of Washington, D.C. were murdered, another 176 were the victims of a sexual crime, and more than 2,000 were robbed. All told that year, an average of more than 11 people in our nation's Capitol were the victim of a violent crime. Every day.

The fact is, we used to have safe streets and sufficient law enforcement. Now, the risk of being a victim of violent crime has risen to deeply alarming levels. We also used to respect and protect private property. Now, shopkeepers and homeowners must fear the mob and pick through the ashes for any possessions left behind. And we used to have a War On Drugs. Now, China and their DINO allies are waging a War *With* Drugs—and Americans are the victims.

The result is communities bordering on chaos, which is precisely the situation Mao and his fellow totalitarians knew would compel people to trade their individual freedoms for collective control.

America is suffering: Our people are being divided, maligned, and mistreated. Our children are being propagandized and preyed upon. Families are fracturing and crime is rising, as our communities are threatened by gutted law enforcement, rising violence, and rampant drug use. All of this is making America's society weaker–but, rather than reverse course, the DINOs are continuing to double down.

Why? Check one:

☐ They are incompetent and don't mean to do this damage.

☐ It's merely a coincidence all this harm is happening now.

☐ They are working to weaken America–*according to plan*.

ATTACKING OUR CULTURAL STRENGTH

"We are called the nation of inventors. And we are.
We could still claim that title and wear its loftiest
honors if we had stopped with the first thing we
ever invented, which was human liberty."

—MARK TWAIN

Nothing has been more fundamental to America's civic culture than liberty. The freedom to believe what we want, say what we want, do what we want, and choose the leaders we want. These freedoms made America what Ronald Reagan called "a shining city on the hill," a beacon lighting the way for all those who want for themselves and their children the liberty that makes this country truly exceptional.

Freedom flows through everything that is distinctly American. When our nation came into being, her birth was announced in a document rightly named the Declaration of Independence. When our Founding Fathers penned the Constitution, they did so to "secure the Blessings of Liberty to ourselves and our Posterity." And when we stand to recite the Pledge, we do so seeking "liberty and justice for all."

Simply put, America's founding was no mere power shift from Great Britain to a bunch of pesky colonists across the Atlantic—it was the birth of a nation never seen before.

To ensure our freedoms would not be in doubt, they were codified in the Bill of Rights and subsequent Constitutional amendments. Unlike so many other people around the world, Americans were free to speak, worship, assemble, publish, petition, and bear arms. Their property could not be searched or seized without cause. They were guaranteed many long-absent legal protections like a speedy trial. And following the Civil War, the sin of slavery was abolished from those states still sanctioning it, as freedom was confirmed for people of all races.

American liberty was such an exception to the global rule, it not only underscored the true meaning of American Exceptionalism but attracted people the world over to leave their homes and legally come here. They fled persecution and war, poverty and want to come to America, and the Land of Opportunity gave them the ability to pursue their own American Dream.

But as previously discussed, it's precisely because of our freedoms that the Pigs are targeting America. We're the gravest threat they've ever faced. A strong America means they have to fight hard for every inch they want to subjugate and enslave. But if they can prevail in weakening America, they'll face no obstacle as they put the world under their thumb.

Whether they are from China, Russia, Iran, or North Korea, are globalists meeting in posh Alpine resorts, or are wannabe autocrats right here in the U.S., their goal is the same: to weaken America and rid the world of the freedoms and opportunity she's given to millions. They seek to deprive Americans of self-determination and instead make us cogs in a collective machine. And they know the only way they can succeed is to weaken America's civic culture by assaulting the foundational pillars on which it stands: our freedoms and Constitutional rights, the practice of our faith, and our participation in the democratic process.

Here's how.

FOES OF FREEDOM

"America is another name for opportunity. Our
whole history appears like a last effort of divine
providence on behalf of the human race."
—Ralph Waldo Emerson

The Spirit of America is simple to understand: it's freedom. Freedom to be what you want, say what you want, worship how you want, think what you want, and do what you want. Our freedom was fought for and secured by courageous men and women who were fueled by a profound belief. Power should rest with the people, not be wielded by so-called "elites."

And that's the rub.

The Pigs think society should be run, well, by them. You see, they and they alone have the expertise and temperament needed to manage human affairs. Yes, this means power must be centralized, but they look at history and conclude it is on their side. Until America came along, autocrats faced no real threat—certainly none with the economic and military might of the U.S. And when America is finally controlled by "elites" who share their world view, this blip on the historical radar screen will vanish.

Step #1 is to impose restrictions on individual liberty, since democracy can be just so *disorderly*. Want to speak your mind? If what you say, write, or post isn't Pig-approved, you'll be hit by the cancel culture, doxed, and deplatformed. After all, if the Left can't ban the ideas they don't like, they'd be forced to defend their own. And given how lousy their ideas generally are, that must be avoided at all costs!

That's why Big Tech platforms censored Joe Biden's critics more than 600 times since the start of the 2020 presidential campaign, according to the Media Research Center. And it's why DINOs tried to establish a Disinformation Governance Board—without a shred of statutory authority—inside the Department of Homeland Security in 2022. DHS, of course, is supposed to be securing our border and homeland, but instead they want it to police Americans' speech. Speech police of any kind is as un-American as you can get, and the placement of this Orwellian "Ministry of Truth" in DHS is particularly damning. Because DHS officials carry guns.

Barack Obama and his Foundation were the orchestrators of this Orwellian tactic. According to *The Hill* newspaper, Obama "convened meetings with academics, activists, media executives and former government officials" to push for this "behind the scenes." Ever the Alinsky-influenced community organizer, he spun the Ministry of Truth as a way to "strengthen democracy." (One imagines he was confident the disinformation board wouldn't inquire about his Obamacare promise that Americans

would be able to keep their doctor and save $2,500 per family.)
In reality, Obama's goal is to delegitimize and silence those not
toeing the Far-Left line.

Such assaults on free speech would create what Thomas
Frank calls "a utopia of scolding in which court is always in
session and the righteous constantly hand down the harshest
of judgments." Obama's Disinformation Governance Board
ran into a public relations buzzsaw, but the effort hasn't ended.
Instead, the White House announced in June 2022 the creation
of a "White House Task Force to Address Online Harassment
and Abuse." What, you might ask, constitutes "harassment and
abuse"? That's for the task force to decide. And since the group
includes the Attorney General and Secretary of Defense, it clearly
has the means to prosecute and punish anyone they decide is
guilty of speech they don't like.

If it is allowed to stand, the Obama-Biden Prude Police is
certain to impose many of the type of sharp contrasts recently
spotlighted by Turning Point USA:

The picture is no brighter for our other freedoms. Want to assemble and petition government about your grievances? Don't be surprised if you're declared a "domestic terrorist," jailed without trial (speedy or otherwise), and aren't able to access your bank accounts. Want to decide whether or not to have a substance injected in your body? Come on, man—it's mandatory vaccines and passports for you. Want to hold onto those guns in your cabinet? Ha, think again!

The fact is, DINOs and their leftist ilk are foes of freedom. Fortunately, we saw them coming a long way away. Back in 1848, Alexis de Tocqueville laid out the dividing line between those who seek freedom and those who seek to destroy it. "Democracy and socialism have nothing in common but one word: equality. But notice the difference: while democracy seeks equality in liberty, socialism seeks equality in restraint and servitude." Indeed.

Take, for example, what the DINOs did with the COVID-19 pandemic. They took full advantage of the Wuhan-sourced virus to rein in our rights and strictly limit our freedom. They decreed we couldn't question "the science" or whisper a word about the virus' origin without being canceled. They ordered us to go home and only emerge if we had masks on our face and a passport in our pocket. They shut down schools, houses of worship, and any business they deemed "nonessential." They appealed when a judge ruled the CDC's mask mandate was illegal, saying it was needed not to protect the public's health but "to protect CDC's public health *authority*." (emphasis added) Any contrary viewpoint was ripped as racist, every Constitutional right was susceptible to suspension, and all restraints on executive actions were disregarded. As Victor Davis Hanson summed it up, COVID "was a rare occasion to leverage agendas that otherwise had no public support in ordinary times."

So much for freedom.

But this assault won't end with COVID. In January 2022, the Biden Administration surreptitiously proposed an amendment to the World Health Organization (WHO) that has the potential to deprive America of its national sovereignty. Considered in May 2022 after only a month of public notice, the amendment was referred to a working group after a grassroots firestorm broke out. But that doesn't mean it is dead—instead, the amendment could resurface as part of a new "Pandemic Treaty."

The reason this is so important is that Biden's amendment would strike the following language from WHO's International Health Regulations: "WHO shall consult with and attempt to obtain verification from the State Party in whose territory the event is allegedly occurring." In other words, striking this language will allow WHO to declare a public emergency on its own and dictate to America how we must respond. Never mind that WHO botched its handling of COVID-19, denying China was the source of the virus blamed for the loss of millions of lives. If Biden gets his way, those same "experts" will have the power to declare as a "public health emergency" anything WHO and its globalist friends want—and *force* us to comply. Vaccinations for all, mandatory lockdowns, social justice 'reforms', restrictions on oil drilling … the list of possibilities goes on. And all due to a stealth amendment from the Pigs in our very own government.

Even as they are gleefully warning of the pandemic's wintertime return, the DINOs are already ginning up the next crisis to leverage against our liberty. (Spoiler alert! The top candidates are economic collapse, food shortages, gun ownership, and "climate crisis.") Like their pals in Communist China, they want to establish a new norm, in which Pigs like them have all the power and the people have none. Forging such upheaval in a place like America isn't easy, but calamities (real or media-hyped) certainly help. That's why they happily adhere to former Obama chief of staff Rahm Emmanuel's rule, "Never let a serious crisis go to waste." Especially when you can create one.

It's also why they've been working so hard to undermine academic freedom. We've already discussed the damage being done to K-12 education by leftists and their CRT/CSE agenda. The situation is just as grim on college campuses. Any student or professor who has the audacity to promote America, discuss our actual (not Zinned-up) history, and seek an open dialogue of alternative views is in trouble. So too are those who dare criticize socialism or invite a conservative speaker to town. They are intimidated, attacked (even physically) and, if at all possible, sent packing.

Freedom of the press is under assault, too, and the perpetrator is often the press itself. Woke culture has invaded newsrooms, with reporters either advancing the Far-Left agenda because they believe in it or because they fear for their careers if they don't. A major media fixation is to divide Americans along racial and gender lines, while another is to convince us our nation is bad and disdained by the rest of the world. The idea is to cause us to believe that, just perhaps, major "reform" is really needed, after all. In doing so, these media hacks are simply following the strategy set forth by Hilary Clinton's mentor and Barack Obama's role model, Saul Alinsky. "The mass of our people," he instructed his followers, "must feel so frustrated, so defeated, so lost, so futureless in the prevailing system that they are willing to let go of the past and change the future."

Fortunately, these Leftists are being met on the media battlefield.

Thomas Jefferson once said, "Where the press is free and every man able to read, all is safe." Helping to preserve that freedom and safety are courageous journalists like James O'Keefe and the intrepid reporters at Project Veritas. In fact, they are doing such a good job the FBI put them under surveillance, according to an FBI whistleblower. Project Veritas' recent exposé about the world of print and social media is especially revealing. In a now-viral video, *New York Times* Pulitzer Prize-winning reporter Matthew Rosenberg admitted that the infamous "pee tape" (yes, the very one Congressional DINOs used in their first effort to impeach President Trump) "of course didn't exist." He also admitted something very important about his woke colleagues. "They're not the majority," he said. Instead, "they're a very vocal, loud minority that dominates social media, and therefore has this hugely outsized influence."

Glenn Greenwald is another model of the courage needed to fight for integrity in journalism. A long-time supporter of liberal causes and candidates, Greenwald also happens to be gutsy enough to tell the truth. He tweeted that the American Left as "an absolutely authoritarian faction" whose "movement is a menace." He has also castigated his former colleagues in the U.S. media for hiding the Hunter Biden laptop scandal, preventing voters from learning more about Joe Biden's corruption prior to the 2020 election. Only in 2022 are *The New York Times* and CNN, among others, finally getting around to this story. But this is not a case of "better late than never." As Greenwald blasted them, sitting on this story was "one of the most successful disinformation campaigns in modern electoral history."

Keri Smith is yet another brave voice against the social justice warriors. Describing herself as a former member of "the SJW cult," she now hosts *Deprogrammed with Keri Smith*, a groundbreaking interview series that reveals how the Left is working to silence free speech, mock faith and family, and eliminate reason. Keri's journey from social justice idealogue to defender of freedom is fascinating. "I eventually got to the point," she says, "where I was more afraid of what would happen if I didn't say something about what I was seeing around me than I was afraid of what would happen if I did say something." Amen.

Adding strength to this truth crusade is the Media Research Center (www.mrc.org), which advances a mission statement I love: "to create a media culture in America where truth and liberty flourish." Their NewsBusters division painstakingly tracks—and exposes—the media's left-wing bias. According to Brent Bozell and his MRC team, media coverage of President Trump was nearly *ninety* percent negative and just *ten* percent positive. Talk about liberal media bias!

And no list could be complete without my friends at Blaze Media. Led by Glenn Beck, the Blaze team defies woke journalism by delivering pro-freedom content on multiple platforms to more than 60 million Americans. Every month! I am so proud to host the Economic War Room show and podcast at the Blaze, especially because doing so enables me to work closely with some of the most stalwart defenders of our great nation, including Glenn, Jason Whitlock, Stu Burguiere, Steve Deace, Pat Gray, Sara Gonzales, and so many more. Another cause for optimism is this: the American people know in their bones that freedom is their right. All signs indicate they won't soon forget what the DINOs inflicted on them during the pandemic. The so-called experts have lost a lot of credibility, making us much less susceptible to the claims of crisis they will doubtless make in the future. Americans also rightly resent the controls placed on them while Pigs partied maskless without any apparent shame. All this sets the stage for a very significant pushback.

Packing a similar punch, Americans are rejecting traditional media in a big way. Reuters Institute surveyed forty-six countries to find which one's media is considered least trustworthy by its viewers. You've already guessed which nation's media ranked dead last—ours. In fact, Gallup reported that just 36% of Americans trust the media to report the news "fully, fairly, and accurately." Similarly, the Pew Research Center asked Americans about social media, and nearly 2-in-3 said it has a mostly negative impact. And more and more people are rejecting the establishment media's leftist bias, as upstart NewsMax draws more viewers than venerable CNN.

So, there is real reason for hope. But if the DINOs get away with pumping up another crisis in their campaign for power, we will lose more of our freedom unless we fight. As Friedrich Hayek summed up the threat, "'Emergencies' have always been the pretext on which the safeguards of individual liberty have eroded."

WHERE COMMUNISM BEGINS

*"Our Constitution was made only for a moral
and religious People. It is wholly inadequate
to the government of any other."*
–John Adams

Put in today's words, President Adams' message is this: if we lose our faith and morality, we risk seeing "consent of the governed" replaced by "control by the governers." No one knows (or wants) this more than the Left. So they long ago realized that, to rid

America of its Constitution and pave the way for Communism, religion would have to go first.

But wait, you may be thinking, what do government and religion have to do with each other? Aren't they supposed to be separated? The answer is yes, but not in the way we've been told.

The very first freedom protected in the Constitution's First Amendment is that of religion: "Congress shall make no law respecting an establishment of religion, or prohibiting the free exercise thereof." You see, America's Founders were men of deep faith, but they were also students of history. They knew only too well that European nations had long waged war in the name of religion. They also knew the problem wasn't religion itself but how governments misused it.

As a result, they set out to do something quite revolutionary— make America a place where people of all religions could practice their faith freely and without coercion by anyone. To grasp how essential that is, recall the photos of Islamic zealots beheading Christians for the "sin" of being Christian. Or Nazis gassing Jews for the "sin" of being Jewish. Not in America. Here, the government would be barred from using one religion or belief to stamp out others. As a result, churches, synagogues, and mosques serve our communities, and their congregants live and work together in peace.

The Founders could have formally established America as a Christian nation, since they and the vast majority of our first citizens were Christians. But, instead, they established America as a tolerant one, consistent with Christian principles. They knew theological divisions would destroy America if they were allowed to fester. And so, the Constitution explicitly prohibits Congress from establishing one religion over others or obstructing anyone's practice of faith.

In other words, the Founders' separation of church and state wasn't to protect the latter from the former but the other way around!

That's not how the Left likes to see it, though. They intentionally mischaracterize the separation in order to rid our society of any vestige of faith. To the Founders, the separation would keep America's future rulers from impeding religion. To the Leftists, separation is a tool to be used to remove religion from our lives. Don't believe it? Just look at the Communists' 28th goal for America:

```
#28. Eliminate prayer or any phase of religious
     expression in the schools on the grounds that it
     violates the principle of "separation of church
     and state."
```

Why does the Left harbor such hatred for religion? Well, consider what George Washington said in his Farewell Address: "Of all the dispositions and habits which lead to political prosperity, Religion and Morality are indispensable supports." *Indispensable supports.* With religion and morality, he knew America would remain free and thrive. Without them, America would be plunged into the division and chaos that open the door to Leftist control.

The data show President Washington was right. Americans who attend services are less likely to be divorced and more likely to be happily married. Religious activity is also linked to lower rates of poverty, drug abuse, crime, suicide, and out of wedlock births. It combats depression, improves self-esteem, and promotes greater physical and mental well-being. And it strengthens individuals' ability to be independent, self-reliant, and less in need of government assistance.

Which, of course, is why the Left works so hard to undermine religion.

In China, for example, the communist government has removed crosses from church buildings, forces missionaries into hiding, and brutalizes Uyghur Muslims on a daily basis. Images of Jesus have been replaced by portraits of Mao and Xi. Statues of Confucius are substituted for those of Buddha. Congregants must register with the police, putting them in dreaded government databases. And China's new director of religious affairs, Cui Maohu, stands accused by human rights activists for brutally persecuting Chinese people of faith. "The CCP considers God its very enemy," explains Marco Respinti of International Family News. "Why? Because God is a direct rival of the CCP."

The Jiangbei Cathedral on fire. Getty Images

For the same reason, Karl Marx famously said, "Communism begins where atheism begins." Marx knew a people rooted in faith is a people raised with freedom. And he couldn't stand that. Nor could Nikolai Bukharin and Yevgeny Preobrazhensky, two Bolsheviks who wrote "The ABC of Communism" in 1920. "We must not rest content with the expulsion of religious propaganda from the school," they warned. "We must see to it that the school assumes the offensive against religious propaganda in the home."

Their comrade, Joseph Stalin, also understood the danger faith posed to totalitarianism, so he held captive and killed thousands of religious leaders while shutting down their churches, synagogues, and mosques. So vicious was his anti-religious campaign, in fact, that the number of churches in Russia collapsed from more than 45,000 at the time of the 1917 revolution to fewer than 500 on the eve of World War II just 22 years later.

America isn't there—yet—but this is exactly the kind of cultural weakening our enemies want.

Knowing the flames of faith must be snuffed out in order for communism and socialism to prevail, the Far Left has steadily worked to separate the American people from the religious principles on which our nation was founded. And as with so many other examples of their plan in action, some of their most notorious efforts began in the 1960s.

In 1962, the U.S. Supreme Court heard the case of *Engel v. Vitale*, in which several Long Island parents challenged the New York Board of Regents' approval of a nondenominational morning prayer in school. The prayer was just twenty-three words in length: "Almighty God, we acknowledge our dependence upon Thee, and we beg Thy blessings upon us, our parents, our teachers and our country. Amen." The prayer was also optional: any student who wished to be excused would be. To the plaintiffs bringing this suit, however, neither the prayer's brevity nor its voluntary nature was good enough. The government needed to step in to prevent its expression altogether. Justice Hugo Black, a former Ku Klux Klan member, agreed and authored the opinion declaring school prayer to be unconstitutional.

Engel v. Vitale opened the floodgates to similar challenges in the succeeding decades. For example, Madalyn O'Hair—who, not coincidentally, was a self-described communist—founded American Atheists in 1963 where she led numerous lawsuits, got Bible reading booted from school, and launched a wave of similar restrictions on the free exercise of religion. More recently, Kamala Harris used her power as California's Attorney General to force companies to comply with government edicts, even when doing so violated their religious beliefs. The Supreme Court blocked her efforts, fortunately, but she tried again as a Senator, introducing legislation that would have done the same thing. To this day, leftist and atheist groups continue to agitate against Americans' free expression of religion, including by athletes and coaches.

During the COVID pandemic, government action against religion took a particularly disturbing turn. Many states and cities forced churches to strictly limit attendance or close their doors altogether, with civil and criminal penalties imposed on any who objected. In Louisville, for example, the mayor banned drive-in Easter services, even though it was obviously impossible for parishioners sitting inside their cars to spread germs. At the same time, casinos, bars, and liquor stores were allowed to continue operating. Revealingly, no public health limits were placed on the Left's crowded street protests, either...

In some states, lawmakers attempted to prevent this double standard. For example, Republicans in Richmond, Virginia (where America's tradition of religious liberty began) tried to pass legislation protecting houses of worship from government-ordered closure. But there as elsewhere, DINOs blocked their path. Similarly, a high school football coach named Joe Kennedy was fired because he had the *audacity* to kneel on the fifty-yard-line for a silent prayer after football games. (Thank God, the U.S. Supreme Court sided with Kennedy in a landmark case brought by my friend Kelly Shackleford and his team at First Liberty Institute.) Or consider the girls on a high school lacrosse team who made t-shirts saying "Pray for Peace" in response to the tragedy in Ukraine. Leftists on their county's school board banned the shirts from being worn—on separation grounds.

Ridiculous! you might say, and you'd be right. But as a result of these efforts, the Left is doing real damage.

A Pew Research Center analysis found that two-thirds of all U.S. adults who regularly attended services prior to the pandemic stopped doing so. Meanwhile, those who say religion plays a very important role in their lives now constitute just 4-in-10 Americans, a decline of more than 25%. And the share of Americans claiming no religion at all has soared more than 80% since 2007, with nearly a third of Americans in that category today.

Additionally, the Left's incorrect interpretation of the separation of church and state has sidelined many in the faith community. As my friend David Barton of WallBuilders points out, America's Founders relied on the powerful messages they heard from the pulpit as they crafted the Declaration of Independence and Constitution. Today, however, few faith leaders speak to their congregations about the important issues of the day. Wonderful exceptions exist, including my friends Pastors Paul Blair and Dan Fisher, but overall the faith community has been engaged in self-silencing. And it is putting our nation at even greater risk.

Benjamin Franklin once wrote, "Only a virtuous people are capable of freedom. As nations become corrupt and vicious, they have more need of masters." On this point, Leftists wistfully agree.

THE END OF DEMOCRACY?

*"Democracy is based on a broad human
aspiration: the aspiration to be heard and
to participate in decision-making."*
—Dinesh D'Souza

But therein lies the problem. What if, as in 2016, the people don't vote the "right" way? What if they vote for someone who wants to put America First? What if they love their country and are proudly patriotic? Or think the government should serve the people rather than the other way around? In these instances, the system may need to be "secured" so such people can no longer use it as they wish. There ought to be a limit to democracy, after all…right?

Well, so the DINOs think. And that's why they took full advantage of the COVID crisis to commit widespread fraud and push election changes that would silence the people. Let's unpack that a bit.

When America was founded, few nations held democratic elections. Today, approximately two-thirds of all countries do. And throughout, this is the way it's worked: an election is held, people (who are alive and eligible) are free to participate, they vote (once), the winners are announced (by official vote counters, not the media), and they serve until the next election. But in 2020, much of that was thrown right out the window for purposes of the pandemic. The tradition of in-person, identity-validated Election Day gave way to mail-in ballots and early voting. All told, more than 100 million votes were cast this way, many of them by dead or incapacited people. At the same time, Silicon Valley tycoons flooded the zone with hundreds of millions of dollars, ostensibly to *fortify* the election. And though the lamestream media keeps repeating there was "no evidence of widespread voter fraud" in 2020, such evidence is stubbornly coming to light—and it tells a very different story.

Former Justice Department official John R. Lott, Jr., for example, conducted a comprehensive statistical analysis that was published in the peer-reviewed journal *Public Choice*. In the six states that proved crucial to Joe Biden's win—Arizona, Georgia, Michigan, Nevada, Pennsylvania, and Wisconsin—Lott examined county databases and found evidence of more than 250,000 excess votes for Biden. Absent these "votes," Biden would have lost some or most of those states, resulting in a Trump victory. Lott's research also discovered that many states didn't check the validity of mail-in ballots. In fact, he found that thousands of people voted in Georgia even though they weren't eligible because they were either unregistered or were incarcerated felons.

In February 2021, *TIME Magazine* published an article that heaped praise on another electoral aberration. Emblazoned with this bizarre title—"The Secret History of the Shadow Campaign That Saved the 2020 Election"—the article said "a well-funded cabal of powerful people, ranging across industries and ideologies, [were] working together behind the scenes to influence perceptions, change rules and laws, steer media coverage and control the flow of information." Put simply, this is the story of Zuckerbucks.

Mark Zuckerberg is world famous as CEO of Facebook/ Meta. Less well known is that he's a harsh critic of President Trump and once fawningly asked Premier Xi to provide a Chinese name for his child. In the months leading up to the 2020 election, Zuckerberg and his wife sent more than *$400,000,000* to the left-leaning Center for Tech and Civic Life. CTCL then distributed the cash to liberal nonprofits and select counties in key battleground states, where it was used to hire and place activists inside elections offices and at polling places. As revealed by Mollie Hemingway, editor in chief of *The Federalist*, the counties that got the most money per voter somehow all tilted in Joe Biden's favor. Huh.

2000 Mules Image. ussanews.com.

And then there is *2000 Mules*, Dinesh D'Souza's astonishing documentary. Following the 2020 election, the integrity group True The Vote bought three trillion cell phone geo-location signals to identify people making the rounds between leftist non-profits and ballot drop boxes. Surveillance videos of those drop boxes revealed something stunning: "mules" (people hired to illegally harvest votes) deposited a total of nearly 400,000 illegal ballots into the boxes—enough to make Biden the winner. Using this data and footage, D'Souza exposed the mules' routes as they returned again and again to the drop boxes, committing election fraud while taking selfies to ensure they were paid.

These documented examples just scratch the surface, but the point they make is clear: despite all the insistence of integrity by DINOs and the media, the 2020 election was indeed marred by widespread irregularities. Rather than be in contention, this conclusion is now widely held. According to a March 2022 Rasmussen poll, more than half of all Americans— including one-third of all Democrats—think "cheating affected the outcome of the 2020 U.S. presidential election." *More than half.* And among those who have seen *2000 Mules*, more than *three-quarters* of them—including nearly seven-in-ten Democrats!—say "the movie strengthened their conviction that there was systematic and widespread election fraud in the 2020 election."

Sadly, that makes 2020 a win-win for America's enemies. For them, cheating in our elections to get rid of an America First president and undermining Americans' confidence in the electoral process is a two-fer.

And they're not done yet. Just weeks after Biden took office in 2021, he issued Executive Order 14019, directing hundreds of federal agencies to "expand citizens' opportunities to register to vote and to obtain information about, and participate in, the electoral process." Though that may *sound* harmless, Constitutional law and election integrity experts warn it's anything but. For one thing, Biden's order imposes federal intervention in elections, which the Constitution clearly made a state matter, and it could link the receipt of federal benefits to election activity. Also troubling, key operatives in the White House are collaborating with far-Left groups like Demos, further amplifying concern this is a deeply partisan activity. And, of course, there's worry that this federal government-wide effort will spend even more money than Mark Zuckerberg did to throw key swing states to the Democrats. Adding weight to such fears is this: the Biden Administration refuses to release information on what it is doing, despite multiple requests from Congress and numerous Freedom of Information Act (FOIA) filings. Clearly, if there were nothing fraudulent going on, they would have nothing to hide.

There are several easy solutions to election fraud, but DINOs unsurprisingly oppose them all. Take Voter ID, for example. Every day, Americans have to show ID to do all sorts of things, like buy a cell phone, pick up a prescription, purchase alcohol or cigarettes, rent a car, board a plane, ship a FedEx package, and donate blood. That's probably why another Rasmussen poll found fully 74% of Americans are fine with requiring voters to show proper identification and think it's "a responsible measure to protect the integrity of elections." Leftists shriek that Voter ID would discriminate against minorities and the poor, but that's not what voters themselves say. Black Americans support Voter ID by a 2-to-1 margin. Those with a high school degree or less support it even more strongly, and Democratic voters themselves favor the idea 59%-to-33%.

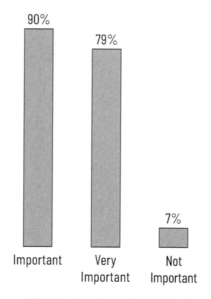

PUBLIC SUPPORT FOR VOTER ID

Source: Rasmussen Reports. National Survey of 1,000 U.S. Likely Voters, conducted Aug. 2-3, 2021.

Voter ID was also endorsed by the bipartisan Carter-Baker Commission on Federal Election Reform in 2005. Comprised of leading Republicans and Democrats—including President Jimmy Carter, former Senate Majority Leader Tom Daschle, and former Congressman Lee Hamilton—the Commission issued a report saying Voter ID was essential to combat fraud.

Native American tribes seem to agree. For example, if you want to vote in a Cherokee Nation election, you have to be a registered citizen of the Cherokee Nation, obtain its official voter ID, and present the ID when you vote. I know because I am a card-carrying citizen of the Cherokee Nation, thanks to my paternal grandfather. Since I've been an at-large voter in tribal elections for the past decade, I also know the Cherokee Nation requires mail-in voters to have their votes notarized. I support all of this because it's simply common sense!

And then there's this: Voter ID also happens to be quite common in Europe, the continent that liberals keep telling us America should be more like. How many of Europe's countries require Voter ID? *Every single one of them!* Our neighbors go even further. Voter ID is required in Canada, and if a voter shows up without one, they can't cast a ballot without declaring their identity in writing and having a poll worker personally vouch for them. Mexico not only requires Voter ID but a thumb print, too, and the thumb print is taken with indelible ink so no one can vote twice!

The people of Arizona apparently think all these countries have it right. During its 2022 session, the Arizona legislature passed H.B. 2492, a measure written by my friend Rep. Jake Hoffman, to implement such common sense protections in the Grand Canyon State. Simply put, the new law ensures ballots cast in Arizona are legal by making voter registration available to anyone who (brace for it) is actually eligible to vote. The horror! All registrants need to do is check a "yes" box indicating they are a citizen and provide some form of evidence in support, like a driver's license, passport, or Social Security card. But that's just too much for Joe Biden, whose Justice Department filed suit against Arizona to block its law. Why does the Far Left oppose something that enjoys such broad, diverse support and would strengthen our elections? Because, as Mark Levin observes, "Marxism does not tolerate the competition of ideas or political parties."

Instead, Leftists seek absolute control over our elections. In order to stifle dissent, they engage in fraud that propels their allies into office. To further rig elections, they open the borders, import millions of grateful people, and make them eligible to vote. To get the outcome they want, they agitate for elimination of the Electoral College, which would enable just a few populous states to choose the nation's President. And to secure all this in statute, they push for HR 1, the laughably named "For the People Act" which would make mail-in voting permanent and prohibit states from requiring Voter ID.

If you think all this is just in time for the millions of Bidenistas crossing our border, you're catching on. Joe Biden's poll numbers are cratering with Americans of Central and South American descent, so his team is flying millions of migrants to towns and cities all over the U.S., giving them cell phones and other free stuff, and grooming them to be pro-DINO voters. This isn't a "conspiracy theory"—it's a fact, and it's happening right now. Take DINO-run New York, for example. The New York City Council passed a law giving voter cards to illegals. They also house illegals in government-owned housing units previously reserved for the city's homeless. Governor Kathy

Hochul then set up an "Excluded Workers Fund" with $2.1 billion in taxpayers' money and paid illegals $15,600 each in unemployment benefits. Guess who they'll vote for?

But that's just the beginning. To tilt Congress in their favor, DINOs also want to grant statehood to DC and Puerto Rico, adding more Democrats to the House and Senate. To ensure their will is done, they seek to "nuke" the filibuster and eviscerate the political opposition's rights, as Senate Majority Leader Chuck Schumer and most of his fellow DINOs tried to do in early 2022. And to prevent the judiciary from standing in their way, they march in front of Justices' homes, plot to "pack" the Supreme Court with more leftists, and try to run Clarence Thomas off the Court.

And they're doing all this with the mega-bucks support of their corporate allies. Wall Street shoveled more campaign cash to Democrats than Republicans in 2020—a lot more. Why? Because it was an investment with the prospects of a very healthy return. As Thomas Frank details in his remarkable books, the Democratic Party has morphed from the party of the people to the party of the plutocrats. He's right. They've been selling out America to Communist China, and since that's where Wall Street parks more and more of its money, Wall Street returns the favor by financing Democratic candidates. So, what we have here is sell-outs contributing to sell-outs, who then clear the path for even more selling-out.

Everybody wins—except the American people.

Free speech is being silenced, freedom of the press is under fire, freedom of worship was shut down, and speedy trials are being denied to those labeled political enemies. Meanwhile, our tradition of free and fair elections is corroded by fraud, which some politicians are trying to make permanent via law. All of this is weakening America's civic culture-but, rather than reverse course, the DINOs are again doubling down.

Why? Check one:

☐ They are incompetent and don't mean to do this damage.

☐ It's merely a coincidence all this harm is happening now.

☐ They are working to weaken America-*according to plan*.

ATTACKING OUR CULTURAL STRENGTH

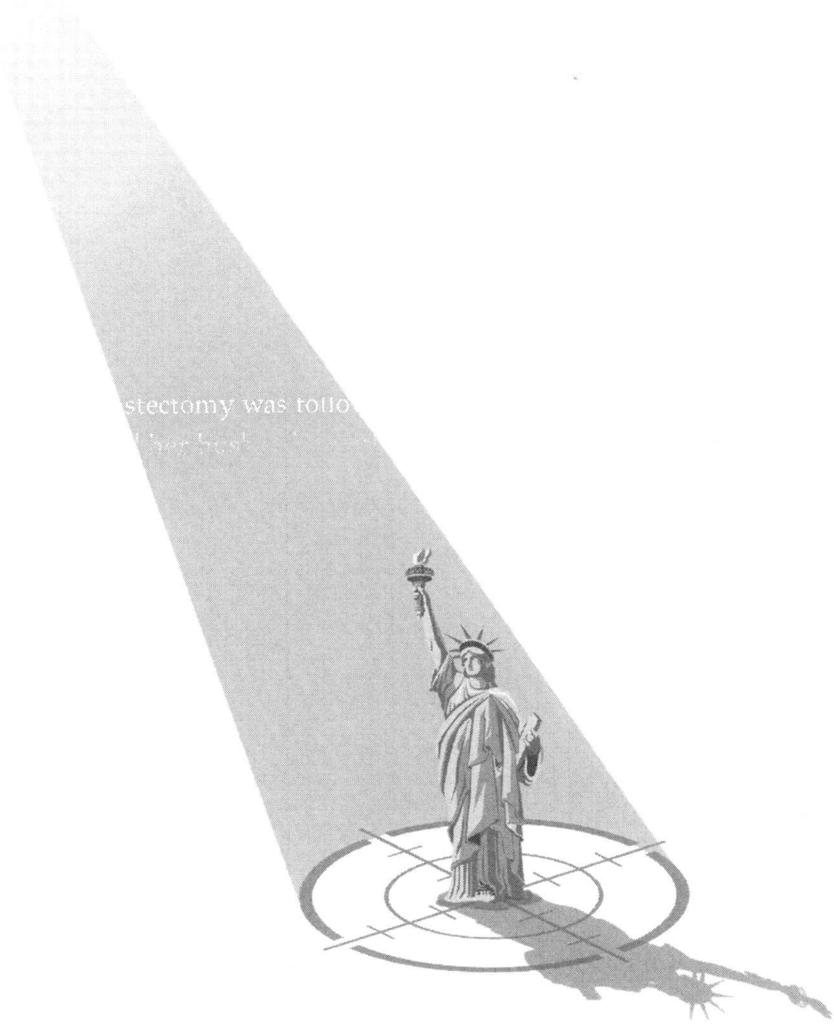

PART IV

PUCK THE PIGS!

> "We the people are the rightful masters of both Congress
> and the courts, not to overthrow the Constitution but
> to overthrow the men who pervert the Constitution."
>
> ### —ABRAHAM LINCOLN

I've got to tell you that when I finished writing Part III, I was mad as hell—and mad at Hell. You might have felt the same way too as you read it. That's because it is now so obvious the Pigs and their autocratic allies are working to destroy the country we love.

They are systematically and ruthlessly undermining the single greatest defender of freedom the world has ever known. They are stalling our economic engine, cutting away at our military might, infecting our society's health, and weakening our cultural heritage. And they are doing all this to secure for themselves the control and cash to which they, as Pigs (both foreign and domestic), have the *audacity* to think they are entitled.

We can no longer shrug away the damage they're doing, dismissing it as incompetence, insanity, or coincidence. We've seen too much to believe that anymore. Instead, we now know America is suffering a multi-front, carefully-organized attack.

SO, WHAT ARE WE GOING TO DO ABOUT IT?

America isn't beaten yet. Not by a long shot. Our people are strong, our love of this great nation runs deep, and we don't lie down for *anyone*. The pain being inflicted by our enemies may yet become even more severe. But this nation has faced grave threats before. And we have overcome every single one.

True, reversing the Pigs' plan won't be easy. Many changes desperately need to be made. For starters, we must restore our foundational freedoms, bring manufacturing jobs back to America, return to energy independence, rebuild our military, reinvest in our police and other first responders, rip CRT and CSE out of our schools, free every child to get a great education, fully secure our border and the integrity of our elections, and send every Bidenista home until they're ready to come here legally. And that's just for a start!

Yet these important and essential changes will be little more than words on paper so long as we continue to be governed by people who are willing to sell out America for power or profit. Simply put, our government must once again be staffed by men and women who are as patriotic as those who built it. And that means the very first job facing the American people is this:

WE MUST TAKE BACK WASHINGTON.

I know that may sound impossible, but it really isn't. There is nothing in D.C.'s air or water that causes Washington insiders to work for themselves—or other nations. It's just that self-dealing and selling-out is permitted there right now.

But it doesn't have to stay that way.

First, *change has happened before*. Precedent can be a big plus, and that's the case here. After Newt Gingrich led the

Republican Revolution of 1994 and became Speaker of the House, he pushed through sweeping reforms that helped make Congress more accountable and transparent than ever before. For example, he opened up committee meetings to the public, established term limits on committee chairs as well as on his own office, and required roll call votes. More needs to be done, and Speaker Gingrich's success paves the way.

Second, *the Pigs are losers.* Go ahead and take another look at the photos of Schumer, Pelosi, Nadler, Schiff, and the others we exposed in Part II. Do you know why they look so familiar? They are a lot like the bossy, annoying, know-it-all teachers' pets we couldn't stand back in school! They simply don't measure up in any respect to the Americans they're supposed to be serving. And they absolutely pale in comparison to our brave men and women in uniform, who truly *are* serving America. In this real-life version of *Revenge of the Nerds*, they wield power over us for the simple reason that we've given it to them. And it's time we take it back.

Third, *we outnumber them.* Joe Biden, Chuck Schumer, Nancy Pelosi, and all their loser friends may seem larger than life, but that's only because their mugs get plastered on TV, newspapers, and the internet by the sycophantic media. In reality, they're small, they're weak, and they're outnumbered.

As an exercise, assume for a moment every single member of Congress, every Congressional staffer, and every federal government employee is an anti-American Pig (and they're not—there are a lot of great patriots in each of those groups). Combined, they number fewer than 3,000,000 people. Now, count everyone else in the U.S., and you get more than 330,000,000 Americans. See what I mean? We outnumber them by *more than* 100 to 1!

U.S. POPULATION AND GOVERNMENT EMPLOYEES

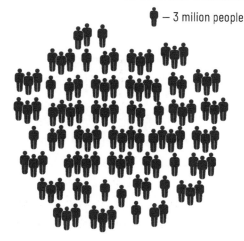

— 3 milion people

Finally, *the Pigs are afraid of us.* They fear the day will come when We The People rise up and reclaim this great nation for *all* Americans. Not only for those with Ivy League degrees, private security, and oceanfront mansions. For the moms and dads who work, raise their kids, go to ball games, and are the people who made this the most productive, creative, and free nation on earth. The Pigs fear that day because it's when all the perks, profit, and privileges they gave themselves will go away.

Folks, that day is NOW.

Alexander Solzhenitsyn once wrote, "Unlimited power in the hands of limited people always leads to cruelty." He was right. And that's why it's high time we put some serious limits on the power we've given the Pigs before they can do even more harm.

Here's how:

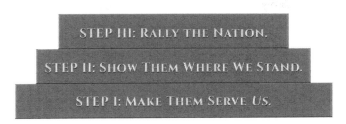

STEP III: RALLY THE NATION.

STEP II: SHOW THEM WHERE WE STAND.

STEP I: MAKE THEM SERVE US.

STEP 1: MAKE THEM SERVE US.

Let's call on every Member of Congress and every candidate who wants to work in Washington to pledge they will vote for a new proposal I call *The SERVE THE PEOPLE Act* (see below). The Pigs will surely gripe about its provisions, even though they're much needed and long overdue. But when they gripe, it will be all the proof we need that they're in Washington to serve themselves—not the people.

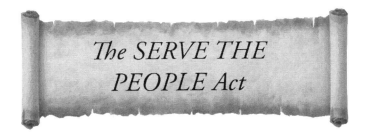

The SERVE THE PEOPLE Act

TITLE I: WORK LIKE WE DO

No American expects to be paid if they don't do their job—unless they work in Washington, that is. Salaries there keep getting paid no matter how little good or how much damage is being done. That's not right, so it needs to be stopped. And the way for us to do that is to institute Pay for Performance for DC (#P4P4DC).

It amazes me that the Pigs think they have the right to assign social and financial scores on *us*. Let's turn the tables on them: #P4P4DC will be the *people's* version of a score for those to whom we give the privilege of serving us. And if they don't measure up, we're not going to pay them. Period.

For starters, the government must be put on a strict diet. With a cap on spending set at a fixed percent of our nation's output, Washington will be subject to a "debt brake" of the type successfully used by Switzerland, Germany, and Chile. This reform mirrors the Maximizing America's Prosperity (MAP) Act proposed by Congressman Kevin Brady and other Republicans, but with a *very* important twist:

- ► Like MAP, *The SERVE THE PEOPLE Act* caps all federal government non-interest spending at a fixed percentage of full-employment GDP, also known as potential GDP. If Washington wants to grow its budget, that's fine—it will just have to grow the nation's economy first. And that means lowering taxes, repatriating jobs, restoring U.S. energy independence, and reversing all the other forms of economic damage described in Part III.

- ► What happens if Washington spends more than allowed by the cap? Here's where the #P4P4DC twist comes in. If spending ever exceeds the cap, across-the-board cuts begin—starting with zeroing out the salaries of the President, Vice President, and every Member of Congress! Only then will Washington learn what everyone else in America already knows: if you want to get paid, you have to *earn* your paycheck.

▶ One more thing: Congress will no longer be able to vote itself a pay hike. (Who else in America can do that?) Instead, if they want to be paid more, they'll have to earn it, just like the rest of us. Specifically, their salaries will only rise by one percent (subject to a maximum ceiling of ten percent) for every one percent reduction in the federal debt *and* one percent rise in America's GDP they achieve. So, if they want a raise, they'll have to deliver results.

TITLE II: LIVE LIKE WE DO

Right now, being a Member of Congress is a pretty sweet gig, particularly because they dig into our wallets for a lot of special perks and privileges. If they get caught sexually harassing a staffer, for example, *we* pay the settlement. We also fork over millions of dollars for their offices, generous health insurance subsidies, travel back home and around the world, lifelong pension payouts, a tax deduction no one else gets, death benefits that far exceed the military's, a private gym with sauna and steam room, free parking spots, and exclusive dining rooms.

As if that wasn't bad enough, lawmakers work fewer days but make a lot more money than the typical American. On average, regular folks will work 260 days in 2022. Judging by its own schedule, Congress was on the job just half that time, thanks to holidays, no-vote days, and "recesses." (Just try asking your boss for a recess from work!) But that doesn't mean lawmakers are paid less than us—not by a long shot. The average salary in the U.S. is around $52,000. In Congress, our representatives' salaries start at $174,000 and reach as high as $223,500 per year (not counting the millions they make from insider trading).

As a result, *The SERVE THE PEOPLE Act* will make Members of Congress live like the American people do:

▶ Their salaries will be cut to zero if they don't do their job (see Title I above).

▶ Their health insurance will no longer be subsidized more than the average American's.

▶ Their death benefits will be reduced to match—not exceed—the military's.

▶ They will pay for parking, gym membership, and meals just like Americans do.

▶ Their number of vacation days will be reduced to match the average American's.

▶ And, if they get caught sexually harassing a staffer, *they* will pay the settlement.

These changes may seem harsh, and even I would be willing to grant lawmakers a perk here and a privilege there *if* they were doing their job. *But too many of them aren't.* Instead, they have allowed— and in the case of many of the crises described in this book, caused—tremendous harm to be done to America. So, if they want their pay, perks, and privileges, they're going to have to *earn* them. How? That's simple.

Stop being Pigs. Start serving the People.

TITLE III: OBEY THE LAW LIKE WE DO

Congress should not be above the law. But that's exactly where they've sneakily placed themselves. Even as they pile heaps of new rules and restrictions on us, lawmakers quietly slip in exemptions for themselves. In fact, laws from which Members of Congress have exempted themselves include— very tellingly—the Freedom of Information Act. Congress also sneaks language into massive bills like Obamacare that waives judicial review—meaning, Congress prevents the courts from being able to review their work and determine if it's appropriate.

To see how wrong this is, read Federalist Paper No. 57. In it, James Madison wrote:

> [Congress] can make no law which will not have its full operation on themselves and their friends, as well as on the great mass of society. This has always been deemed one of the strongest bonds by which human policy can connect the rulers and the people together. It creates between them that communion of interests and sympathy of sentiments of which few governments have furnished examples; but without which every government degenerates into tyranny.

Madison was exactly right, so *The SERVE THE PEOPLE Act* will apply to Congress every law it imposes on the American people. It will also empower the people to sue the government if it ever fails to comply with the laws and regulations it creates. But that's just the start. The Act will also include additional overdue reforms to clean up Washington:

► It finally puts an end to insider trading by Members of Congress and their families. For years, lawmakers have misused their positions to score huge profits on Wall Street. No longer. *SERVE THE PEOPLE* gives them 6 months to divest their holdings or put them in a blind trust. It requires full disclosure and audits for compliance. And it forces them to forfeit to the American people via the Treasury any profits they make in violation of this reform.

► It closes the revolving door that has allowed profit to compromise public service. For too long, our representatives have sold us out to secure high-paying jobs following retirement. *SERVE THE PEOPLE* puts a stop to that by prohibiting lawmakers, officials, and staff from ever lobbying for a foreign client, imposing a 10-year delay before they can be a lobbyist or board member for a U.S. entity, and banning them from negotiating those jobs while in office.

► It stops the corrupt practice of lawmakers getting money from special interests, too, which often results in their passing laws that benefit those interests—not the American people. Instead, *SERVE THE PEOPLE* bars Congressional incumbents and candidates from accepting any federal campaign contributions from a lobbyist or any other employee of a lobbying firm. They are also prohibited from fundraising of any kind during Congressional working hours.

► It makes it *crystal clear* that selling out America to our enemies will be a punishable offense. Section 2381 of U.S. Code Title 18 defines treason as when someone "owing allegiance to the United States ... adheres to their enemies, giving them aid and comfort within the United States or elsewhere." *SERVE THE PEOPLE* updates the definition of "adheres" to include directly investing in, lobbying for, or receiving funds from a foreign nation, company, or other entity.

► Finally, *SERVE THE PEOPLE* ends the era of career politicians. Many lawmakers and officials stay in office for decades, which makes elections uncompetitive and stifles new ideas for America. As a result, the Act sets a sensible term limit of eighteen years for anyone wishing to serve in Congress or the federal bureaucracy. After all, if they haven't done what they came to do by then, they're probably not the right person for the job.

TITLE IV: JOIN THE ELECTORAL CLUB

As discussed earlier, Voter ID is the unanimous norm throughout Europe. Closer to home, it's also required by our neighbors, Canada and Mexico, which add further safeguards like written declarations of identity and thumb prints using indelible ink. Voter ID is overwhelmingly supported by the American people, including minority voters. It also ensures any American citizen who doesn't have an official ID is able to get one for free.

And yet, for reasons we already know, the DINOs are trying to institutionalize fraud in America's elections. *SERVE THE*

PEOPLE will thwart their plans by establishing common-sense safeguards for election integrity:

- ► It has America "join the electoral club" by applying Voter ID rules here that are already in use around the world. Specifically, official federal, state, local, or tribal photo identification proving a person is a U.S. citizen will be required before they can register to vote, receive a ballot, or vote in a federal election. *SERVE THE PEOPLE* also empowers states to require anyone registering to vote to provide evidence of citizenship.

- ► It puts an end to non-citizens registering and voting in our elections by requiring the Department of Homeland Security and Department of Justice to share information about anyone who has illegally registered for or voted in a federal election. All who are found to have done so will be investigated for violation of federal law and, if guilty, have their visas revoked, their citizenship applications rejected, and a seat on a return flight home.

- ► It improves the ability of those defending America to participate in our elections. Towards that end, *SERVE THE PEOPLE* requires the Department of Defense to make voter registration offices and assistance available on all military installations for military personnel and their families. It also permits veterans groups to conduct nonpartisan voter registration drives at commissaries and other appropriate military post and base sites.

► It strengthens state election officials' ability to confirm that a voter is a U.S. citizen by giving them secure access to Department of Homeland Security and Social Security Administration databases. In addition, *SERVE THE PEOPLE* ensures state officials are notified by federal courts whenever anyone is excused from jury duty for not being a U.S. citizen, even though they appear on voter rolls, and it requires an investigation of those suspicious circumstances.

► Last but by no means least, *SERVE THE PEOPLE* adds important anti-fraud measures to mail-in procedures. Anyone who registers by mail will have to submit a copy of their ID and cast their first vote in person where they will present their ID, unless they are in the uniformed services, posted overseas, or covered by the Voting Accessibility of the Elderly and Handicapped Act. Anyone voting via absentee ballot must also submit a copy of their ID.

TITLE V: CHECK YOUR WORK

Can you imagine handing in a project to your boss or teacher that you never even bothered to review? Me either, but members of Congress do a version of that all the time. Specifically, they routinely vote on bills they haven't even read, despite the fact more than 4-in-5 voters think that's a terrible idea. Sometimes, they just don't want to be bothered with reviewing legislation before they foist it on us, but more often it's because they were not given sufficient time to do so. That's what happened with the 5,000-page government spending bill passed in 2022, which lawmakers were given less than twelve hours to read.

This means members of Congress are not doing a key part of their job, and it results in bad bills becoming bad laws and rules we must then live with forever, often at tremendous cost. According to the Mercatus Center, America's economy would be at least 25% larger—meaning American families would be earning thousands of dollars more every year—if the impact of federal rules had simply remained constant since 1980. Instead, Congress' passage of unreviewed legislation has caused the mountain of federal rules to grow much larger, placing an enormous burden on our productivity.

Ronald Reagan once quipped, "The closest thing to eternal life on earth is a government program." So, shouldn't Congress at least ensure those programs, not to mention all the other laws and rules it creates, benefit our country? I think so, and that's why *The SERVE THE PEOPLE Act* includes reforms to improve the work being done in Washington:

► It ensures Members of Congress have enough time to review legislation before voting on it. Like Senator Rand Paul's *Read the Bills* proposal, it gives lawmakers a period equal to one legislative day for every twenty pages in a bill. In cases of emergency, this can be waived if four-fifths of all Members agree. But otherwise, *SERVE THE PEOPLE* puts an end to the practice of rushing through burdensome legislation without at least reading it.

► It establishes a new sunset rule: every law, regulation, and government program must be reviewed and reapproved once every five years. If Congress fails to review one or doesn't reapprove it, it will be automatically canceled. This compels lawmakers, officials, and bureaucrats to ensure all laws, rules, and programs are delivering a positive outcome for America. And it ensures that all that don't will be history.

With these reforms in place, Washington will once again help rather than harm our nation. And that's likely the reason why Washington won't want to touch *The SERVE THE PEOPLE Act*. After all, too many Washington insiders don't want to work like the American people do, and they certainly don't want to live like we do. Many also don't want to obey the law like we do, join the electoral club, or check their work. So, they'll do their very best not to vote on this proposal—unless they're forced to.

That's where all of us come in.

The fact is, most politicians try to avoid political risk any way they can. So, we have to make it clear to them their political careers will be over if they don't act on these reforms. How? By rising up and making a lot of noise!

Fortunately, making yourself heard is easy: simply scan the QR code below and take just 1 minute to join a nationwide grassroots action campaign calling on every federal lawmaker and candidate to pledge they'll vote for *The SERVE THE PEOPLE Act*!

Now, I know you may be thinking any promise these people make won't account for much—and when it comes to many of them, you'd be right. That's why we're not urging lawmakers and candidates to simply make a *verbal* promise they can easily forget or pretend was never uttered.

We're calling on them to sign their name to a written pledge. After all, if our Founders were willing to risk their lives, fortunes, and sacred honor by signing

SCAN ME

the Declaration of Independence, today's politicians should put their names on the line, too.

If they truly want to lead and support our country, politicians will unhesitatingly put its interests at the top of their list. As a result, how they react to our demand for reform will tell us a lot about who they really stand with: the American people— or the Pigs.

If they sign and act on this pledge, they'll earn and get our support. If they don't, they'll get our boot.

STEP 2: WEAPONIZE YOUR MONEY.

As covered in Part III, big Wall Street firms are pushing woke investment via ESG. Their claimed objective is to protect the Environment, promote Social justice, and provide good Governance. But in reality, ESG doesn't do those things. Instead, it weighs down American companies with woke requirements— like ending fossil fuels—that are not being applied to China.

Why is Wall Street demanding one thing of America while giving a free pass to China? Because many of Wall Street's elites have been so corrupted by Communist China they see no problem with this hypocrisy. Just as galling, China is terrible at E, S, and G! They're among the worst polluters on the planet. They repress their people with social credit scores, slave labor, and live organ harvesting. And their governance solely benefits the big-wig bosses in the CCP.

And yet, Wall Street is funneling our money into China without one moment's regard for its ESG record.

This may enrage you, and it should. But it shouldn't surprise you. After all, many on Wall Street are just like the other Pigs exposed throughout this book. They are cashing in while selling us out. They are hurting America while helping China. And they are using our money to finance China's rise while hastening America's decline.

No more. It's time for us to stand up to the elites and take back our country. Fortunately, we can do this with two simple steps.

First, express your righteous anger. In the 1976 movie *Network*, frustrated Americans threw open their windows and yelled "I'm mad as hell, and I'm not going to take it anymore!" Thanks to modern technology, you can make your voice heard even louder and more easily than that. Just scan this QR code or type MadAsHellCampaign.org into your browser. That will take you to a grassroots campaign where, in just 60 seconds, you can tell Washington to put an end to Wall Street's hypocrisy.

Second, retake control of your money so it will stop being used to fund the Chinese Communist Party and its attacks on America. Start by telling your financial advisor you want China out of your portfolio. If he or she refuses, find an investment advisor who's pro-America, not pro-China, and who will make sure your investments are, too. After all, having a patriotic adviser by your side can make all the difference.

If your adviser wants to help but doesn't know how, nominate him or her for training at the National Security Investment Consultant (NSIC) Institute. This online training course teaches advisers about the economic war we're in right now, how woke Wall Street is, and the dangers of China's threat. It will help them protect your portfolio during turbulent times and show them how you can weaponize your money to fight

back. Just as important, it provides a powerful alternative to ESG investing: Liberty, Security, and Values (LSV), which ensures our money is invested to defend—not harm—America.

Just scan this QR code or type NSIC.org to get started!

STEP 3: RALLY THE NATION.

On June 6, 1943, 160,000 Allied troops under the command of U.S. General Dwight D. Eisenhower landed on the beaches of Normandy and parachuted into the French countryside. Thousands died that day as they launched the fight to free Europe, but their sacrifice was not in vain. Within three months, their incredible bravery led to the Nazis' retreat across the Seine and marked a vital turning point in the war against National Socialism.

Since then, every American has commemorated D-Day as a sacred day in our history. Every American but Joe Biden, that is. During the first year of his presidency, D-Day came and went without a single word from the White House. June 6, 2022 almost passed the same way, too, until a social media firestorm forced his press office to issue a tweet … at 8:45pm.

Biden may not want to call attention to America's heroic fight for freedom against socialism, but we sure can—and we must.

To save America, we need to make it clear to the Pigs we are not beaten, and we refuse to give up our country without a fight. We will not kneel, we will not give way, and we will never surrender. Instead, we will stand up, take action, be heard, and save this great nation. President Reagan once asked, "If not us, who? If not now, when?"

The answers are clear: US and NOW.

Fortunately, there's a great way we can rise to this challenge: *display the American flag!* Fly it from your front porch, stick it on your car or truck, wear it proudly as a t-shirt, button or hat, or show our colors any other way you prefer.

Just imagine what America will look like when all of us fly her flag. Like you, I still get choked up when I see the Stars and Stripes. I love the ceremonies that precede sporting events. And I smile whenever I see someone's house or car proudly adorned with red, white, and blue.

I also get some satisfaction imagining the response of those Leftists who hate our country and flag. Take the Pima County Democratic Party, for example. Rather than honor America's Independence, it tweeted an invitation to a July 4, 2022, event called "F*ck the 4th" (and without the asterisk, too). Or consider Kristin Pitzen, a high school English teacher in southern California (of course) who said she took down the American flag "because it made me uncomfortable." Now imagine the Pima County Democrats and Ms. Pitzen *surrounded* by American flags. It'll probably make them mad, but it will make the rest of us feel patriotic as all get out.

So, please fly or otherwise display our flag **within a week** of reading this. And then keep doing so! If you need to order one, there are a lot of great options including the VFW Store, which donates a portion of every sale to Veterans of Foreign Wars (VFW). To reach their site, simply scan this QR code:

In addition to flying the American flag, urge our fellow Americans to "ChooseFreedom"! This is a new

SCAN ME

initiative launched by some wonderful patriots, and it's spreading the "ChooseFreedom" message across America on banners, car flags, bumper stickers, clothing, cups, and more. It includes local events, called Freedom Parties, and features some of America's leading influencers. It promotes ChooseFreedom crowdfunding campaigns to support pro-freedom groups and initiatives. And

it includes grassroots action to support pro-freedom reforms like *The SERVE THE PEOPLE Act*.

If you want to take part, scan this QR code to learn more about ChooseFreedom, order a banner, shirt or sticker, and see where a Freedom Party will be taking place near you!

OUR TIME IS NOW

On October 30, 2008, Barack Obama haughtily previewed what would begin the following week. "We are five days away," he vowed, "from fundamentally transforming the United States of America." Millions of voters cheered his message, thinking it promised a post-racial future in which the nation's first black President would close the chapter on racial tension and open the door to a new era of unity, freedom, and opportunity for all.

But now we know that's not what he had in mind at all.

Consistent with Communist Rule #15—"Capture one or both of the political parties in the United States"—Obama and his fellow DINOs have completed the Far-Left's takeover of JFK and Barbara Jordan's Democratic Party. With the exception of the four years in which Donald Trump unexpectedly disrupted their plans, Obama, Biden, and their fellow DINOs have been engaged in transformation of the most evil kind. Like the Pigs and globalists with whom they closely align, America's Far-Left is determined to weaken this great nation militarily, economically, socially, and culturally. And in the interest of installing themselves as America's ruling elite, they have inflicted the damage exposed throughout this book.

It's infuriating to take it all in, but we must. Just since Obama's 2008 election, the Pigs have tripled government debt to over $30 trillion, terminated our energy independence, and shipped U.S. jobs overseas. They ordered "nonessential" small businesses and churches to close, ballooned the welfare state, broke the food supply chain, and unleashed rampant inflation. They erased the southern border, allowed lethal drugs and terrorists to flood in, and slipped illegals into the heartland via ghost flights. They slashed and shamed our military, abandoned our allies, and aided our enemies. They corrupted our children at school, used race and gender to divide us, imposed disproven vaccine and mask mandates, and spurred a wave of suicides. They defunded the police, decriminalized lawlessness, and unleashed a shocking wave of violent crime. They engaged in systemic election fraud, jailed their critics without trial, and tried to impeach President Trump not once but twice. And on top of all that, they *criminalized* America's foundational freedoms of speech, religion, and assembly.

We can no longer shrug off these crises as the result of incompetence or mere coincidence. Because they are neither. As we now know, all of this is happening *according to plan.*

The America we love is under attack. And the DINOs aren't going to stop until they complete their takeover of our country.

But they've made one very big mistake: *they have completely underestimated the American people.*

We are not stupid, we're not sheep, and we certainly aren't deplorable. Quite the contrary. We are a proud, innately decent people with a deep sense of right and wrong. We are also powerful and have what it takes to defeat the Axis of Authoritarianism once and for all. And thanks to America's Founders, we know just how to do it:

> *Governments are instituted among Men, deriving their just powers from the consent of the governed … whenever any form of Government becomes destructive of these ends, it is the Right of the People to alter or to abolish it, and to institute new Government, laying its foundation on such principles and organizing its powers in such form, as to them shall seem most likely to effect their Safety and Happiness.*

We, the American people, have *not* consented to what the DINOs are doing to our country, so it is up to us to end the destruction they've caused. Barack Obama may have vowed to fundamentally transform our nation. But America survives and, when we mobilize, she will be saved.

By defending liberty, we will ensure America remains the world's beacon for freedom and opportunity. And by taking a stand against those who seek to destroy America, we will be standing up for the values and freedom that made her the greatest country ever created.

So, enough with Obama's "transformation." ***The restoration of America begins now!***

Passing *The SERVE THE PEOPLE Act* is just the start. So, too, is weaponizing our money, proudly flying our American flag, and telling Washington we ChooseFreedom. But, just as the Founders did two and a half centuries ago, we must start somewhere.

Let's make that start. ***Today.***

ABOUT THE AUTHOR

Kevin D. Freeman, CFA is considered one of the world's leading experts on economic warfare and financial terrorism. He has consulted for and/or briefed the U.S. Congress, the Intelligence Community, the SEC, and the Departments of Defense, Homeland Security, and Justice on his extensive research about Global Economic Warfare.

He is a co-founder and host of the Economic War Room on BlazeTV (EconomicWarRoom.com) and of the National Security Consultant Institute (NSIC.org). Kevin also serves as a Senior Fellow at the Center for Security Policy and author of the blog GlobalEconomicWarfare.com.

His first book on economic warfare, *Secret Weapon*, became a *New York Times* bestseller and his second, *Game Plan*, became an Amazon bestseller.

ACKNOWLEDGEMENTS

I would like to gratefully acknowledge the following, without whom this book would not exist:

My Economic War Room co-founders and partners, Mike Carter and Russell Lake, and their families. Also to the silent partner who believed in us at the beginning and has supported us throughout.

Bill Blankschaen and the talented team at StoryBuilders who helped shepherd this book from burning desire to finished work and my friends at AlignAct.com, who are giving every American the tools we need to save our nation.

The NSIC Institute (including the advisors and supporters) and LibertyHawk Ranch (yes, you Van!).

The prayers of many great friends, our Corporate Chaplain Keith Green, and prayer warriors around the world who have gone to their knees for America and for Liberty.

Our visionary Founders and the courageous men and women whose sacrifices over the centuries made it possible for Americans to be free.

The patience, love, and support of my wonderful wife and best friend, Marnie Freeman, and the understanding and joy of our two beautiful, wise, and strong daughters.

Most of all, I wish to thank the Lord Jesus Christ who came to set at Liberty those who have been captive. To Him be all glory, honor, and praise.

ACCORDING To PLAN

SPREAD THE WORD!

We must inform our fellow Americans about the plan to destroy our country.

Not long ago, America was a very different country. Freedoms were protected, streets were safe, families were whole, and the future looked bright. Schools delivered a quality education, Made in America meant something, and people came to our country—legally. Gas was cheap, jobs plentiful, and our government wasn't bankrupt. In those days, America came first, unity and faith were honored, patriotism was a virtue, and the police were funded.

Today, however, so much is going wrong.

Schools are failing our children, replacing education with indoctrination. Crime, drug use, and suicide are all on the rise. Government debt and inflation are skyrocketing too, as high gas prices and supply shortages make the American Dream harder to reach for millions of families.

Meanwhile, our oil fields are closed, but the border is wide open, destroying jobs and allowing millions to enter illegally. Our military is weakened by budget cuts and woke culture. We retreat from enemies, leave weapons in the hands of extremists, and are led by politicians who profit from America's foes.

And our deep commitment to community is now fractured by race divisions and social justice discord. The fundamental freedoms of speech, assembly, and commerce are being restricted, and our right to choose how we live is denounced by so-called experts who impose rules they themselves disregard.

Some say all these problems are happening because our leaders are incompetent. Others think it's merely a coincidence. But to millions of concerned Americans, those explanations no longer ring true.

We now know these problems are happening *according to plan*. And we also realize this plan *will* succeed—unless we unite to save America.

For the sake of our country's future, please share this book, give copies to your family and friends, and invite others to do the same!

Visit AccordingToPlanBook.com or scan the QR code below and take just 1 minute to join the movement. Together, we can save the great nation we love!

Made in the USA
Columbia, SC
10 October 2022